Ridolfo Capoferro's

The Art *and* Practice *of* Fencing

A Practical Translation for the Modern Swordsman

• Complete English Translation • Practical Action Synopses
• Historical Notes • Glossary • Original Illustrations

Tom Leoni

Freelance Academy Press, Inc.
www.FreelanceAcademyPress.com

Freelance Academy Press, Inc., Wheaton, IL 60189
www.freelanceacademypress.com

Printed in the United States of America
by Publishers' Graphics

20 19 18 17 16 15 14 13 12 11   1 2 3 4 5

ISBN 978-0-9825911-9-2

Library of Congress Control Number: 2011937159

To the memory of my grandfather, Attilio Bellot,
an extraordinary man.

Contents

Acknowledgments

I would like to extend a big thank you to Mr. Guy Windsor of the School of European Swordsmanship (Helsinki) and Maestro Sean Hayes of the Northwest Academy of Arms (Eugene, OR) for their kind and thorough peer-review.

I would also like to warmly thank Mr. Devon Boorman, head of the Academie Duello School of Modern Swordplay in Vancouver, BC, for supplying the plates from his original copy of the *Gran Simulacro.*

Foreword

In retrospect, it is entirely fitting that I met Tom Leoni at the same event where my interest in Capoferro was first ignited. Watching him teach a class on my favourite treatise of the 16th century, Viggiani's *Lo Schermo,* was a treat, the words of the treatise brought to life with an unmistakably Italian flair. And fencing him was equally rewarding—everything he was doing was clearly based on his main source. It was like fencing the book itself. Since then, his efforts in this field have set the standard for rendering Italian treatises into English—perhaps the most important historical swordsmanship publication of the last five years being his sterling rendition of Fiore dei Liberi's *il Fior di Battaglia.*

With the present book, Tom completes the Holy Trinity of early 17th-century rapier: monumental Fabris, practical Giganti, and now at last the legendary Capoferro. Fabris defines the boundaries and structures of the Art, albeit with some wild mechanics thrown in. Giganti offers us an excellent, straightforward training syllabus of the main actions. Capoferro lies somewhere in between: he gives us a complete theory of the Art and a fairly comprehensive Practice, offering a vital third window into this system.

As a rapier teacher, and Capoferro specialist, I have been longing for a readable, usable, accurate translation of *Gran Simulacro* to be published. So much so that I almost mortgaged my life away to buy an original of the treatise last year, with the intention of producing a translation with copies of the plates myself. I know enough about the process of executing a good translation to have been hugely relieved to hear from Tom that he was doing one himself. And what a book! The volume you are now holding is a vital contribution to the study of historical swordsmanship in general and 17th-century Italian rapier in particular. I wrote up my training method for my interpretation of Capoferro to create a bridge between beginning rapier practice and working directly from the treatise—it's just easier for most people when everything is explained in modern terms. I expect this translation to become the keystone of that bridge—a vital step for those wanting to work with the source directly but lacking the language skills to do so. By including a blow-by-blow walk-through of each technique as well as an extensive glossary of rapier fencing terms, Tom has perhaps even made my book superfluous!

There is no substitute for training with sharp swords. There is no substitute for the experience of having someone trying to kill you with a sword. And there is no substitute for working with the original source material. But all of these should be worked up to (or in the case of the second, avoided altogether!) and for fencers wanting an authoritative English rendition of one of the most celebrated treatises of all times, this volume is as good as it gets. For researchers wanting help figuring out some of Capoferro's more abstruse (dare I say baroque?) linguistic constructions, this volume is indispensable. No fencing library is complete without it.

Guy Windsor
Helsinki, July 2011

Introduction

Making Capoferro Accessible to the Modern Rapier Student

It is an honor to offer my own understanding of the words of the great Ridolfo Capoferro to the English-speaking audience. His treatise, from which I have learned at least thirty percent of what I know about rapier, is incalculably dear to me. Other good translations of his work exist, both in print and online, and with this translation I don't mean to second-guess any of them. What has moved me to complete and publish this book were primarily three things:

1. The desire to render Capoferro's rapier treatise (as I understand it) absolutely clear in modern English, through a faithful rendition of both the technical content and the nuanced style of this important author
2. The desire to offer synoptic snapshots of all the actions Capoferro illustrates, so as to facilitate understanding, learning and practicing his repertoire sword-in-hand
3. The desire to offer a basic glossary of rapier fencing terms tied to specific examples from an authoritative treatise like Capoferro's

Even while being a few centuries far removed, martial-arts treatises such as Capoferro's are still excellent instruction tools. Their language is studiedly plain and direct, their terminology fairly (although not always) consistent, and their description of the art sufficiently complete for us to garner a good idea of how our ancestors fought and fenced.

The task I proposed to myself with this book was to clear this direct line—from the modern student to the ancient text—as much as possible. My hope is that rapier students with a grasp of the fundamentals can follow his words without much trouble, and practice the wonderful art he describes without needing a purely interpretive work as a go-between.

So, I have striven to offer as precise and clear a translation as I could, paying special attention to technical content, style and tone. And I have also offered practical synopses of each of the action plates, to summarize in a schematic, easy to follow fashion the vast fencing repertoire that Capoferro presents—as well as a glossary with examples from Capoferro's theory and plates.

If there are any mistakes in this book, they are mine and mine only. I hope that my decades-long commitment to Italian rapier has minimized the possibility of there being too many. Be as it may, I also hope you'll look kindly on my effort to bring you this master's words in English, as I have had the joy of "tasting" them in the original language . . . which happened for the first time in a most unexpected place.

A Personal Journey

Together with Salvator Fabris' *Scienza d'Arme* (1606) and Francesco Alfieri's *La Scherma* (1640), Ridolfo Capoferro's *Gran Simulacro dell'Arte e dell'Uso della Scherma* (1610) was the first Italian Renaissance fencing text to ever find its place on my desk. And actually, it had been the one I was most eager to receive. To properly explain why, I need to take my reader on a brief journey back to the modern dark ages of the days before the Internet.

Growing up in Northern Italy, around museums and collections, I had nurtured from an early age a passion for ancient swords and edged weapons. Once in my twenties, I decided to deepen this passion by finding period documentation about the actual use of these weapons, and in particular, of the fascinating sword we call "rapier." The problem I was trying to solve was this: I knew there were 17th-century texts outlining the use of the rapier, but I had no idea of who had written them or what their titles were. One day, I therefore decided to head for the library, as a first step on this new journey. Good move, say you? Bear in mind, this was not Padua, Venice or Milan, but the "city where the West begins"—my undergraduate Alma Mater town of Fort Worth, Texas. My first few trips were frustratingly unsuccessful, to the point that I was getting ready to give up. But upon my last attempt, almost by accident, I happened upon a copy of Jacopo Gelli's *L'Arte dell'Armi in Italia* (1906), a survey of Italian fencing literature from the first extant medieval documents to the writer's days.

I eagerly thumbed through this book's first few chapters, where I learned truly marvelous things (or so I thought then). I learned that a medieval master by the name of Fiore de' Liberi had introduced twelve guards that would remain the mainstay of Italian fencing until the 18th century; that longsword fencing required extraordinary strength given the colossal weight of the weapon; and that 16th-century masters from Bologna, with colorful names like Marozzo and Manciolino, did not teach fencing, but only "tricks and stratagems learned throughout their adventurous lives." Truly eye-opening information, I thought. This man is not only giving me the facts I wanted, but is also telling me what to think about them. Perfect. And then I turned the page leading into the section about the 17th century.

That section was nothing less than a celebration of one name: Ridolfo Capoferro. Ridolfo Capoferro, the oasis of forward-thinking science in the barbaric desert of mankind's infancy (also known as the 1600s). Ridolfo Capoferro, the man who invented the lunge, the parry, the cavazione, the concept of defense, the concept of offense, and who determined the proper length, weight, and balance of the sword to boot. Ridolfo Capoferro, the author of "such a perfect work, although nearly three centuries old." I had struck gold. I elegantly unsheathed one of the 3x5 index cards I was carrying, and, in as much of a majestic hand as I could muster, I penned "Ridolfo Capoferro: *Gran Simulacro dell'Arte e dell'Uso della Scherma,* 1600.[1] Best."

Ever the heretic, however, I kept reading forward, and learned a few other names of published 17th-century masters. Thus, on the opposite, non-ruled side of the card, I scribbled two other names and titles: "Salvatore Fabris, *Scienza d'Arme*; Francesco Alfieri, *La Scherma*. Maybe worth a look."

I still have that index card, which I ironically keep in my bound copy of Alfieri's scans. I say ironically, because, according to Gelli's summary five-line paragraph on Alfieri, this master's single contribution to Italian fencing had been to "not quite stand in the way" of the art's evolution.

A few months later, the library scans of the three works had arrived. It was summertime and I was still in college, so I had time to pore over the texts to my heart's content. Having three of them at the same time was a true bonanza. It allowed me to compare their definitions of *common* concepts, to note the fact that they were undoubtedly describing a *common* style, and to even start learning the first *common* fundamental actions they outlined and illustrated. Common traits make the study of any discipline easier.

Gradually, I summoned up the analytical skills I had learned in early-music school (music and fencing being both active arts), and my reading turned into deeper and deeper study. The loose pages of the three treatises became arranged in increasingly smaller piles which proliferated first on my desk, then on the floor adjacent to it, and finally in my whole study. The dozens of Post-it notes of different colors marking them and sections within them gave the room the surreal look of the geometry of the fields of Kansas as viewed from an airplane window. My journey into Italian rapier history had begun, and under what auspices!

---

1 As we will see later, this is the publication year alleged by Gelli, which is ten years earlier than the actual date of publication of the treatise's first known edition (1610).

What did strike me, however, was that I did not see such a difference in quality between these three texts. Among them, the treatise of Fabris stood out as the most complete, the most clearly written, and best organized; but the other two I also found (and still find) to be incredibly valuable windows to a Renaissance sword-art as taught and practiced in its apogee. Even more puzzling was to find—in his own printed words—that Alfieri had a high opinion of Fabris, but a not-so-good one of Capoferro. Was Gelli wrong?

Fast forward two decades, and I now find myself in the position to write about Capoferro. Capoferro is perhaps the most loved name in the historical rapier-fencing community, with Fabris a very close second, also largely because their lavishly-illustrated works have been both translated into English and therefore made available to a wide audience. But does Capoferro deserve this place of honor—a place of honor not quite reserved for masters like Giganti, Alfieri, Marcelli, Pallavicini, di Mazo and others?

Who was Ridolfo Capoferro?

The very little we know about Capoferro comes from his treatise, contemporary literature and Victorian scholarship. His treatise, published in Siena in 1610 by Silvestro Marchetti and Camillo Turi, is an oblong small quarto, bearing the frontispiece *Gran Simulacro dell'Arte e dell'Uso della Scherma di Ridolfo Capo Ferro da Cagli, Maestro dell'Eccelsa Natione Alemanna, nell'Inclita Citta' di Siena. Dedicato al Serenissimo Sig. Don Federigo Feltrio della Rovere Principe Dello Stato D'Urbino* (Great representation of the art and practice of fencing by Ridolfo Capoferro of Cagli, master of the most high German Nation in the noble city of Siena. Dedicated to the most serene Sir Don Federigo Feltrio della Rovere, prince of the state of Urbino).

The inscription in the master's portrait re-states that he was *calliensis*, from Cagli, and that he was fifty-two years old at the time of publication, placing the date of his birth around 1558. Cagli is a town in the Marche region of Italy, approximately one hundred miles due east of Florence, and currently in the provinces of Pesaro and Urbino. That his book was published in Siena, and that he is identified as operating as a master in Siena strongly suggests that it was in this Tuscan town that he plied his trade.

The first question surrounding him has to do with the statement *maestro dell'eccelsa Natione Alemanna*—master of the most high German Nation. Was he in fact German or of German origin, perhaps his last name being a translation or a variation of a German name? Occam's Razor would suggest it. However, he identifies himself as being from Cagli, and in chapter one, when talking of fencing in his day, he counts himself among the Italians ("we Italians carry the torch of fencing"). A second option would be that he was the fencing master of a German fraternity or group situated in Siena, which could be what the *Natione Alemanna* was. With the international nature of late-Renaissance commerce, study, and travel, this is a viable possibility, although it is a point that bears much deeper study.

Even within his treatise, his name is spelled both Capo Ferro and Capoferro. I strongly prefer the latter spelling, also because Capoferro (or Capoferri) is a rather widespread last name in the area between southern Lombardy and Rome. This is also how his name appears to be spelled most consistently in contemporary literature. According to the Heraldry Institute of Rome, the origin of the name Capoferro (spelled as one word) is from the Capoferri family of Rome, which among other personages produced a *condottiero* who served Caterina Sforza.[2] Whether this is the same branch of the family as our fencing master's I cannot say with any degree of certainty.

To see who Capoferro was and how influential his martial writings may have been, we have to widen our "concentric circles" and see what has been written about him from his day forward.

2 Online searches by last name on the Heraldry Institute of Rome Web site may be performed at http://www.heraldryinstitute.com.

The Two Faces of Capoferro: Period Literature versus Victorian Scholarship

Together with the Liechtenauer school of 15th-century Germany, the best-documented among the major historical-fencing traditions is what we now call the Italian "rapier school" of the 17th century. The amount of consistent and mutually corroborating data points we have about each tradition makes the job of the modern martial-arts researcher[3] much easier.

Among the features that started appearing in 17th-century Italian fencing texts—sometime around mid-century—were references to past masters. First, these references appeared as loose comments interspersed among the pieces of instruction. Then, towards the last quarter of the century, some authors started including a separate section on the recent history of fencing, complete with a list of notable works. From these, we can obtain important information about what past treatises would have been known or may have been still in circulation in the late 1600s.

Although it may be tempting to read too much into the comments by one period master about another, a fact stands out. References to Capoferro by 17th-century Italian masters who followed him chronologically are either negative or neutral.

For instance, on page 20 of his 1640 treatise *La Scherma*, Alfieri stated that Capoferro's opinion that the *prima* and the *seconda* are not true guards was "badly conceived," even spelling the master's name, perhaps with a deliberate touch of malice, as *Capo di Ferro* (literally, "head of iron"). While also disagreeing with Fabris on some issues, he made it a point to do so respectfully, calling Fabris "the grand master" and "a man of the greatest name in our discipline."

A few decades later, Giuseppe Morsicato Pallavicini included a history of fencing in his treatise *La Scherma Illustrata* (1670). Capoferro's name and treatise appear on the list, but without the positive comments reserved to other masters. We find a similar situation in Francesco Antonio Marcelli's *Regole della Scherma* (1686), where the author listed most works known (or known of) in his time, heaping praise on some of them—most notably Giganti and Alfieri. But here too, nothing but a short, neutral mention of Capoferro and the *Gran Simulacro*.

Meanwhile, Fabris' style had taken Northern Europe by storm after his teaching first at the court of the Archbishop of Bremen, then at the king of Denmark's. In his 1677 German edition of Fabris' work, Johann Joachim Hynißsch, the editor and translator, chronicles the rise of Fabris' art in German circles—calling it first *italienische Fechtkunst*, then giving it a less nationalistic flavor and naming it *Salvatorische Fechtkunst*. Even Gerard Thibault of Antwerp, writing a monumental treatise instructing in the Spanish style in the 1620s, had devoted a chapter on how to defeat Fabris' students, in one of the first inter-stylistic notes that would become the mark of French smallsword treatises a few decades later.

So, there is plenty of documented praise of some masters, with relative silence about Capoferro—at least as far as my research has shown to this point.[4]

3 I use the word "researcher" in its loosest and most unpretentious meaning, although professional scholars are starting to show an interest in these arts.

4 I am in the process of compiling a list of references to Italian masters by foreign authors, beginning in the 16th century. This list is far from complete, and I therefore do not discount the possibility that I will find (as I hope) some mentions of Capoferro's work.

Jacopo Gelli: The Main 19th-Century Source on Capoferro

Italian fencing historian Jacopo Gelli (1858–1935) is an important reference for the students of Capoferro. Not only did he provide copious information on Capoferro and his treatise, but may have been the original source of the enthusiasm that continues today surrounding the rapier master from Cagli. Before him, British historian Egerton Castle had also written a sentence in praise of Capoferro, but it is with Gelli that the veritable posthumous cult of this master begins.[5]

The most frustrating aspect of researching from Gelli's writings is the fact that seldom—if ever—does this historian provide references for his statements or findings. And given the fact that a few of his pronouncements are demonstrably dubious (some of which I recounted above), it feels irresponsible to take all his information at face value. Yet, it would be equally irresponsible—indeed, perhaps more so—to be skeptical of all of his research, both in terms of its factual content and in terms of the perceptions that it created or amplified through some rather charismatic editorializing.

Before I relate what Gelli writes on Capoferro, I must present an important piece of information, which will put many of Gelli's words into context. In the later part of the 19th century, the Italian fencing community was embroiled in a bitter *querelle.* One camp was partial to the Northern Italian school, also called "mixed" because of its French influence; this style was embodied by the teachings of Giuseppe Radaelli. The other camp took the side of the Southern or Neapolitan school, which they viewed as pure and quintessentially Italian. What had started as an academic divergence of opinions exploded into outright cold war after the Italian government appointed a Neapolitan, Masaniello Parise, to head the prestigious Scuola Magistrale in Rome in the 1880s.

Jacopo Gelli, a Northerner, took the side of the Radaellians and their mixed school. And as a recognized authority on fencing writing influential texts, he would not pass on the opportunity to delve into fencing history and re-emerge with some convenient pieces of evidence that would settle matters definitively in favor of the mixed style. This is one of the reasons why, with just a concatenation of a few ideas, Gelli jumps from the 17th century to his day to praise the mixed school or to heap scorn on the Neapolitans. In all this, unfortunately, Capoferro, Fabris, Alfieri, and contemporaries get caught in the crossfire.

In his *Bibliografia Generale della Scherma,* Gelli begins his entry on Capoferro by stating that the 1610 Siena edition, widely recognized as the first even in his day, must have been preceded by an earlier one.

> "This [earlier] edition," says Gelli, "we do not see mentioned in any other fencing bibliography or treatise. The certainty that this edition predates the cited one [i.e., that of 1610] may be deduced by irrefutable material proof. We have in our possession 28 plates of Capoferro [...] that are not the same as those of the 1610 treatise, since the text describing the actions is not printed on the opposite side of the plates, but rather below them. [...] That the 1610 edition is the second and not the first is evidenced by some, so to speak, graphical matters. The plates we have are much better drawn and reproduced than those of the 1610 Siena edition; not only that, but the ornaments and the landscapes forming the background to the actions in various plates are not present in the Siena edition by Marchetti and Turi.
>
> "[...] Plate 8 of our collection has as a sea harbor as a background, complete with ships, which is not the case in the 1610 Siena edition. Lastly, Plate 4 shows the Biblical Deluge as a background, which is not found in the aforementioned treatise."[6]

---

5 In his 1885 work *Schools and Masters of Fence,* Castle states on page 107: "none ever had such a share of fixing the principles of the science" as the treatise of Capoferro.

6 Jacopo Gelli, *Bibliografia Generale della Scherma, con Note Critiche, Biografiche e Storiche,* Florence, 1890, pp. 45, 46. All translations are mine unless noted otherwise.

In other words, Gelli was not in possession of a frontispiece that positively dated this set of plates. Furthermore, the Brera library in Milan has a copy of Capoferro, dated 1629 and printed in Siena by Ercole Gori, where the plates match exactly the description that Gelli gives of this supposed earliest printing: they are indeed of better quality, and they are complete with text under the illustrations, a sea harbor with ships in Plate 8 and the Biblical Deluge in Plate 4.

Was a set of loose plates from this 1629 edition what Gelli had? Perhaps, perhaps not, but in the words quoted above, I see no compelling indication of why he would think it *must* predate 1610. I remain therefore thoroughly unconvinced of Gelli's "irrefutable material proof" that an earlier edition existed, also because no such edition has surfaced in the last 100 years. In any case, Gelli dates this "earlier edition" to 1600 in his 1906 book *L'Arte dell'Armi in Italia*. This is stated as fact with no further explanation, evidence or caveat.

Another piece of circumstantial evidence against Gelli's chronological theory is the dedication of the *Gran Simulacro*, which Capoferro dated April 8, 1610. The dedication is to Federico Ubaldo della Rovere (1605–1623), although Capoferro addressed this to his father, Francesco Maria, as Federico was only four years old in April of 1610. Since Federico was not even born in 1600, the dedication of the 1610 edition would not be the original one, if we are to believe Gelli, but a rewrite to a new patron. This, in my opinion, is highly unlikely.

In any case, after gifting Capoferro's treatise with ten extra years of vintage, thereby placing it before the important 1606 works of Fabris and Giganti, Gelli is free to ascribe to Capoferro a list of "firsts." Among them, here is what he says on Capoferro's dividing the sword into forte and debole:

> "In fencing, the introduction of the theory of the grades of the blade is of such great importance that it revolutionized the old way of fencing, it disclosed new horizons and it allowed our art to make a giant step on the road to progress. So, deservedly, Capoferro can be called he who regenerated Italian fencing, and Italian fencing owes him a very great debt."[7]

Then, after the statement that Capoferro recognizes six guards—whereas he mentions seven—comes the connection with the *querelle*; here is where Gelli presses Capoferro into the service of the 19th-century mixed school.

> "The lunge in Capoferro is practically the same as that executed today in the mixed school. But what a difference, if we compare the lunge of Capoferro with that [...] of the Neapolitans, or that of the Parise school! The latter especially, if you put it side by side with the fencing in Capoferro, you would think you are looking at a *rickety pygmy* next to a most perfect *giant*."[8]

Besides these editorials, complete with italicized emphasis, Gelli gives us some information that, if reliable, is undoubtedly of great interest. Firstly, the authorship of the plates. According to Gelli, and to Castle before him, the engraver used by Capoferro was a Raffaele Schiamirossi. My research has not yielded any other evidence concerning this. However, I have found a Raffaele Schiaminossi (1529–1622?), an engraver mentioned in Didier Bodart, *The Zanchi Collection*, Rome (De Luca), 1985. The dates make it plausible that the engraver would be the same, although by 1610, he would have been of a rather mature age.

The second and even more interesting piece of information given by Gelli is that the copy of the 1610 edition of Capoferro in his possession bears the inscription,

7 Jacopo Gelli, op. cit., p. 47. Even assuming the chronology proposed by Gelli, the author fails to recognize that much earlier authors like Di Grassi had introduced the gradation of the blade (see Giacomo Di Grassi, *Ragione di Adoprar Sicuramente l'Arme*, 1570, p. 28), which Gelli knew because he mentions it elsewhere in his works.

8 Jacopo Gelli, op. cit., p. 47.

> "under Plate 1, and in Capoferro's own handwriting: 'So that the sword may be easily handled and well balanced, you must ensure that the blade, when mounted, does not weigh more than 15 ounces, the hilt 10 and the pommel 12. This way, it will be light and well fitted'."[9]

As is so often the case in Gelli's writing, there is no reference as to *why* he thinks the handwriting must have been Capoferro's. My educated guess comes from reading his later work, *L'Arte dell'Armi in Italia*, where on page 104 he claims to own Capoferro's handwritten draft for the 1610 edition. Still, even if it is a generic 17th-century hand, it is a matter of great interest to know that someone must have considered that particular weight to be the ideal specification for a sword used in the style we call "rapier."

In *L'Arte dell'Armi in Italia*, Gelli keeps celebrating Capoferro, whom he claims as publishing in 1600. He concludes the chapter on Capoferro by stating that the master from Cagli was "the author with the most ample horizons, between the 17th century and today, and it is to him that we owe much of the progress that the art of arms has made in the last three centuries."

He even grudgingly justifies the excellence of the seminal 1803 Italian fencing treatise by Giuseppe Rosaroll Scorza and Pietro Grisetti (both Southern Italians), by claiming rather petulantly and arbitrarily, that these two authors did nothing but "copy Capoferro."[10]

Gelli's works being quite influential on subsequent historical fencing research, it comes as no surprise if the name of Capoferro came to be associated with absolute excellence, from the last century up to our day.

Now, the question is, did Gelli merely give Capoferro the long-overdue praise that his contemporaries denied him? Undoubtedly, he did so to some extent. But it is also difficult to refrain from looking at Gelli's findings with some skepticism. There are, for instance, the reading mistakes. How could such a champion of the treatise miscount the number of guards that Capoferro uses? Then, there is his unscientific approach to the treatise's first printing date, which allows the crediting of Capoferro with so much innovation, let alone the fact that many of Capoferro's supposed "firsts" can be found in much earlier works. Lastly, of course, there is the *querelle*-driven agenda behind so much of Gelli's words.

If so many of the premises for Gelli's conclusions rest on shaky ground, should we still look at the laurels he placed on Capoferro's brow as deserved—laurels that, to this day, survive indirectly through the myriad of secondary sources citing or relying on Gelli? When historical research crosses so far into editorializing, it is tempting for subsequent generations of researchers to pile on more layers of counter-arguments, to impute motives, and to look at the discipline more as rhetoric than as science—meanwhile losing sight of the actual object of our research. So I'll check myself, close the book on Gelli, and focus on Capoferro, which is a treasure trove of vital information for the fencing historian.

Capoferro, His Treatise and Its Importance to the Modern Student

Capoferro's treatise is entitled *Gran Simulacro dell'Arte e dell'Uso della Scherma*, which I have translated as "The great representation of the art and practice of fencing." The conceptual pair of *arte* (art) and *uso* (practice) occurs quite frequently in Renaissance literature, the former referring to a discipline's rules and pedagogical principles, the latter to its practical application. Here, for instance, is the entry for *arte* in the influential *Vocabolario degli Accademici della Crusca*, 1612:

> "ART: Derived from experience, it is the use of reason to tackle any matter, as is the case with the seven liberal arts and the mechanical arts. Latin *ars*.

9 Jacopo Gelli, op. cit., pp. 44, 45.

10 Jacopo Gelli, *L'Arte dell'Armi in Italia*, p. 114.

> "Albert[i]. c. 46. Arts serve Nature, and knowledge rules them. Art comes from the Latin *arcere,* which means to force or constrain. Art is a finite disposition of infinite things. Put another way, art is a collection of rules all aimed at the same end. Knowledge of all things can be obtained through practice [*uso*], and what man knows, he knows through either art [*arte*] or practice [*uso*]. Likewise, arduous strain satiates man, while sleepless art often gives him great riches. Apply yourself to study, so that you may learn the art, whose rules will help your mind as practice helps your hand: art gives, while practice has. If you join art and practice, a difficult journey will appear short."[11]

Accordingly, Capoferro divides his treatise into two main sections: the art (pages 1 to 24) and the practice (pages 25 to 121). In the first section, he distills fencing down to a finite set of rules, describing the goal of fencing, the ideal guard, the ideal posture and mechanics of the body, the concepts of fencing time and measure, and the principles of offense and defense. In the second, he gives what would be best described as a thorough survey of the terminology, concepts, actions, and repertoire that were practiced and taught in his day. It is also in this second section that he inserts 43 plates illustrating guards, the lunge, and a vast number of actions with the single sword, sword and dagger, sword and cape, and sword and a large round shield or *rotella*.

The apparent contradictions between the rules he gives in the first part and the actions he describes in the second are easily explained. In the first part, he presents the art as it should be. In the second, he lists and describes what is commonly practiced, even when it strays from the confines of the platonic ideal of the art.

One of the puzzling aspects of Capoferro concerns the guards. Like most Italian masters of his time, he uses and describes the *prima, seconda, terza* and *quarta* (first, second, third and fourth) as the mainstay of all positions and actions.[12] However, he also introduces, without explaining their nature, a *quinta, sesta* and *settima* (fifth, sixth and seventh), the latter not even illustrated. In the action plates, the last three guards get barely a mention, which makes it even more puzzling as to why he would go through the trouble of illustrating two of them. Throughout the whole Italian rapier literature of the 17th century, these guards occur only in Capoferro.

Besides the way he presents his material, and the aforementioned three guards, there is nothing truly unique about Capoferro's treatise—which I consider an eminently positive point. The style he describes is typical of the Italian tradition at the beginning of the 17th century, making the *Gran Simulacro* one of the most valuable data-points for understanding historical fencing in Baroque Italy. While giving preference to the single-tempo actions also favored by Fabris, Giganti and Alfieri, and employing mostly the hand-positions and guards of prima, seconda, terza, and quarta, he also makes use of the two-tempi parry-riposte and occasionally resorts to guards best known from the preceding century's tradition—such as the *guardia di testa* and the *guardia di faccia.*

The repertoire is also typical of the time, and wonderfully rich. Actions generally start with one of the contenders gaining the opponent's blade, to receive a cavazione or a feint by cavazione accompanied by either a lunge or a left-foot pass. In turn, the cavazioni are defeated by counterattacks in single tempo, by voids, by parries and ripostes using either edge of the sword, or by other actions of the blade or the companion weapons. Of particular note is an outside circular parry against an inside attack, which Capoferro calls *affrontare la spada*; this precedes a low-line riposte to the flank (e.g., plates 13, 14 and 17).

Capoferro uses mostly the seconda for actions to the outside and the quarta for actions to the inside, as is to be expected from a rapier master. Occasionally, cuts such as mandritti, riversi and stramazzoni are used instead of thrusts, again, very much in line with the tradition of the time, as are grapples, disarms and dagger-thrusts.

Although the master belittles the feint in the first section of The Practice, he thankfully makes wide use of it in the action plates—the feint being one of the true pillars of Italian rapier fencing. We find a similar

11 Leon Battista Alberti (1404–1472), a gifted Italian linguist, philosopher and architect, was one of the authors quoted in the *Vocabolario.*

12 For a basic explanation of these concepts (and others found in this chapter), please see the glossary at the end of the book, or just below under "What You Need to Know to Tackle Capoferro."

incongruity with the technique of gaining the sword, as well as with the use of the dagger; actually, Capoferro ends up being second only to Fabris among masters from the early 17th century as to the amount of ink he devotes to this companion weapon.

These are the slight incongruities within the text that, in my opinion, prevent this treatise from being objectively viewed as the uncontested crown jewel of the rapier age. Also, the organization of the *Gran Simulacro,* compared to other treatises, seems less logical, and the writing not always as tight as it could be. With regard to the first issue, an obvious example is the author winding his way through sword and dagger actions, then sword and cape, only to return to sword and dagger without any apparent reason. As I mentioned before, the *quinta, sesta* and *settima* guards are only named in passing, with no indication of whether they are just sword and dagger guards, as it would appear, and no description of their nature.

As for his writing, Capoferro did not always achieve the *chiarezza* (clarity) that distinguishes an otherwise superior and truly brilliant pedagogical work. Punctuation is often haphazard, lists of points he announces then get lost in a haze of words and ideas,[13] and even terminology is at times ambiguous. For instance, in chapter IV (paragraph 46), he states:

> "Wide measure is that distance from which I can strike the opponent by performing an *accrescimento*[14] with the right foot; and this is the first narrow measure."

This leaves the researcher with the task of understanding what he really means.[15] And lastly, for "gaining the sword," he uses a variety of synonyms that have confused readers who may not have thoroughly digested several fencing treatises of the time in the original language.

Despite the fact that it would have benefited from a stronger editing hand, Capoferro's treatise, if properly understood, is a treasure for understanding the art of the rapier. My personal favorite is his description of the guard and the elements within it, which is the most thorough of any period treatise I have ever analyzed. Regardless, the sheer amount of mechanics, theory and definitions it gives, together with a rich amount of fencing repertoire with a variety of weapon-combinations, makes it a resource whose worth to today's serious rapier student is inestimable.

Language, Translation, and Editorial Decisions

Besides the elevated dedication, Capoferro's writing is expectedly in the plain style, which at the time was considered ideal for imparting instruction. His pages occasionally contain humor, adages and other accents that offer a window into the heart of the author; most of all, it is Capoferro's passion for his discipline and for teaching that comes through in some rather moving swells throughout the text. His Italian is perfectly in line with his times, meaning that there are no affectations or archaisms in his sentences. The erudite references to Aristotelian concepts, Latin passages, and historical facts are woven into the texts quite naturally, without resulting in something stylistically or thematically out of place.

I have striven to translate his style as well as his words as accurately as possible into English, leaving nothing to ambiguity save for when the master is himself ambiguous. I have kept the footnotes to a minimum, only employing them when I thought they would convey something of essential value to the reader. I have also translated the terminology in a way that is as clear and consistent as possible, so as to make the technical content clear. To help with this, I have included a practical synopsis of the actions of each plate, as well as a glossary at the end of the book.

---

13 See Chapter V, Tempo.

14 An *accrescimento* is a forward motion of the front foot, as happens in a fencing lunge.

15 Here is the most likely interpretation. Wide measure: the distance from which I can reach the opponent by means of an accrescimento or lunge. First narrow measure: the distance from which I can reach the opponent *after* performing an accrescimento or lunge.

Since in some of his action plates he addresses the reader in the second person, I have used that person throughout, to make reading smoother and more consistent. Also, in the practical synopses of the plates, I have decided to call the fencers "agent" and "patient," to avoid adding more letters or numbers to the reading. I have intended "agent" to mean he who moves first, "patient" the one who has to react, regardless of who receives the hit at the end of the action.

Hopefully, this translation will shed even more clarity on the work of this key rapier master, and the synopses of the action plates will spur students of historical fencing to practice, enjoy and memorize the wonderful repertoire in the *Gran Simulacro.*

What You Need to Know to Tackle Capoferro

This section is meant to serve as a short, standardized primer on common principles in Italian rapier—as applied to practically all written instruction from the early 17th century. Please bear in mind that the following assumes a right-handed fencer. As an additional resource for understanding commonly-used rapier fencing terms, please refer to the glossary at the end of the book.

What sword to use – Use any sword commonly referred to as "rapier." This is a single-handed, straight-bladed, two-edged sword with a hilt of varying complexity that enables you to place your index finger around the ricasso, i.e., the thick section of the blade just beyond the cross-guard (more on this in the section about gripping the sword). As for length, any well-balanced rapier whose crossguard stands as high as your navel will give you good results. I refer to the rapier as "sword" throughout the translation, since this is how Italian masters call their weapon (*spada*).

Division of the blade – The blade is divided in two equal halves: *forte* (strong) and *debole* (weak). The forte is the half closest to your hand and is used for parrying. The debole is the other half and is used for the offense. Some masters divide the blade in different ways, but this will suffice. The blade also has a true edge and a false edge. The true edge is the edge facing the ground when you carry the sword sheathed at your side.

How to grip the sword – Grip the sword with your whole hand around the handle, and the index finger through the *incascio*.[16] Let your relaxed thumb rest on the tip of the index, achieving the grip called *a chiave serrata* (close-keyed) by Italian masters.

The four hand-positions – The four hand-positions or guards in Italian rapier are (assuming a right-handed fencer and the sword-point aimed at the opponent):

- The *prima* (first): hand at shoulder-level or higher, palm facing right, the sword's true edge pointing up
- The *seconda* (second): hand at shoulder-level, palm facing down, the sword's true edge pointing right
- The *terza* (third): hand lower than the shoulder (chest-level or lower), palm facing left, the sword's true edge pointing down
- The *quarta* (fourth): hand lower than the shoulder (chest-level or lower), palm facing up, the sword's true edge pointing left.

The three bastard hand-positions – These are the intermediate positions between prima and seconda (called therefore *prima-seconda*), between seconda and terza (*seconda-terza*) and between terza and quarta (*terza-quarta*).

16 The *incascio* is the portion of the hilt between the front arm and the ricasso.

Capoferro's other guards – The *quinta* (fifth), *sesta* (sixth) and *settima* (seventh) are peculiar guards used, as far as my research has shown so far, only in the *Gran Simulacro*. Even within this book, they only receive a passing mention and are therefore not as crucial for the understanding of the text as the aforementioned prima, seconda, terza and quarta.

Other guards mentioned in the book are the *guardia di testa* (head guard) and the *guardia di faccia* (face guard). The first is formed by extending your sword- or dagger-arm forward towards the opponent's head, hand palm-down, orienting your blade up and obliquely to your forward-left (with the sword) or to your forward-right (with your dagger); this makes it ideal to parry cutting attacks to the head. The second is formed by turning your sword- or dagger-hand palm up, with your arm and weapon extended towards the opponent's face and forming a single straight line; this makes it ideal to parry attacks to the face.

How to stand in guard – The main guard is the initial position in rapier fencing, and it should be practiced to become second nature, since it is the "neutral" position from which all other actions spring. The general Italian guard (terza) I teach is as follows:

- Start by standing erect looking at the opponent, your chest facing left, your right foot pointed at the opponent, your left foot pointed to your left and slightly back, forming with the right foot an obtuse angle, heels touching. Have your sword at your left side, as if in a scabbard; hold it against your hip with your left hand on the blade just under the hilt; and grip the sword with your right hand as described.
- "Unsheathe" your sword and point it at the opponent's face, with your hand in terza, your arm quite extended (but never locked) and your hilt approximately at the height of your solar plexus.
- Bring your front foot approximately one-and-a-half shoe-lengths forward along the same straight line between you and the opponent, right knee almost straight. Keep most of your weight on the left foot by gently bending your left leg and slightly tilting your body back, chest still facing left. Hold your head also slightly back, looking squarely at the opponent, your neck relaxed.
- At the same time as the last point, extend your relaxed left forearm towards the opponent, with your hand open but relaxed and your palm facing the opponent; there should be approximately a span's width between your arms.
- You should end with your left shoulder, knee and toes aligned on the same vertical line (similarly to line A-B-C in Capoferro's plate 5). Your hilt and your right foot should be on the same vertical line, and your heels on the same line that goes between you and the opponent.

How to advance and retreat – In Italian rapier, you can advance and retreat in three main ways (I'll describe only the advance—for the retreat, invert the instructions starting with the opposite foot):

- With gathering steps, i.e., by bringing the left foot close to the right, then moving the right foot forward by the same distance, which makes you end in the same stance as when you were in guard.
- By bringing your right foot between a half and a whole shoe-length forward, then bringing your left foot forward by the same distance, which makes you end in the same stance as when you were in guard. This is the one I teach first, and the one that has given me the best pedagogical results.
- With passing steps, i.e., by bringing your left foot forward ahead of the right (toes still pointing left), then bringing the right foot forward ahead of the left by the same distance (toes still pointing at the opponent), which makes you end in the same stance as when you were in guard.

Inside line and outside line – These are the two main lines in Italian rapier, and are used for attacks to the chest, face or head. Inside: when you and your opponent are in guard or execute an action and your opponent's sword is to the left of yours, you are both to (or on) the inside. Outside: when you and your opponent are in guard or execute an action and your opponent's sword is to the right of yours, you both are to (or on) the outside.

Low line and high line – These are the other two lines in Italian rapier. Low line: the line used for attacks to the flank (i.e., lower torso) or leg. High line: when the opponent lowers his weapon into the low line and you execute an action to his chest, face or head, you are using the high line.

Lines in sword and dagger (or cape, rotella) – The lines with sword and dagger (or other companion weapon) are not defined as consistently. The most commonly-used lines are above the sword, below the sword, between the weapons, above the dagger and below the dagger. The terms "inside" and "outside" are used more rarely, since the weapons are two (outside the sword would be different from outside the dagger, for instance).

The lunging thrust – From the guard, quickly extend your sword-arm straight towards the opponent, then violently bring your body forward with a simultaneous forward motion of the right foot. Recover by pulling back your head and torso first (bending the left leg during recovery facilitates this), then your right foot, then and only then your sword. A lunging thrust to the inside ends with your hand in quarta; one to the outside, in seconda. Other hand positions are used by Capoferro for more specialized situations.

Gaining the opponent's sword – Gaining the opponent's sword means situating your weapon in such a way that he cannot perform an offensive action without changing lines by means of a *cavazione* (see "cavazione" further down).

This action is performed almost always with the true edge. When you gain the opponent's sword to the inside, your hand is in quarta or terza-quarta, your blade crosses over the opponent's (forte on debole) and your sword-point is directed above the opponent's right shoulder. When you gain the opponent's sword to the outside, your hand is in seconda or seconda-terza, your blade crosses over the opponent's (forte on debole) and your sword-point is directed above the opponent's left shoulder.

On whichever side you gain the opponent's sword, you are satisfying these four conditions:

1. The point of intersection of the blades is closer to your hilt than to his (forte on debole)
2. Your blade is above his
3. Your sword crosses over his and remains pointed in the vicinity of his silhouette (point in or near presence)
4. If he attacks with a thrust without first changing lines with a cavazione, you have in effect "pre-parried" his thrust.

Note: early-17th-century Masters such as Capoferro, Giganti and Fabris advocate performing this action with little or no pressure against the opponent's blade.

Note: the two positions you use to gain the opponent's sword to the inside and outside are the basis for the position for the inside and outside **simple parries** (parries without a simultaneous counterthrust). The only difference is the degree to which you may have to move your weapon to either side, so that you may safely set aside the opponent's attack.

The cavazione and half cavazione – A *cavazione* is a thrusting attack that is preceded by or incorporates a spiral motion around the opponent's weapon to free your sword while or after the opponent gains it. In other words, it is a thrusting attack with a line-change. Cavazioni can proceed inside to outside (and vice-versa) and high line to low line (and vice-versa). A half cavazione in Italian rapier is mainly one that starts from the inside or outside lines and ends on the low line.

Use the hand (i.e., the joint of the wrist) to perform this action, not the elbow or the whole arm. Cavazioni can be performed under or above the opponent's sword or dagger—Capoferro generally specifies when to use one or the other.

Which hand-positions to use – Following is how you should keep your hand in Capoferro—and in the greatest majority of Masters in the Italian tradition:

- When standing in guard, keep your hand in terza
- When gaining the opponent's sword or performing a simple parry to the inside, turn your hand in terza-quarta (Capoferro implies a quarta with his letters, D in this case)
- When gaining the opponent's sword or performing a simple parry to the outside, turn your hand in seconda-terza (Capoferro implies a seconda with his letters, B in this case)
- When performing a thrusting attack or counterattack to the inside, turn your hand in quarta
- When performing a thrusting attack or counterattack to the outside, turn your hand in seconda

Cuts – Cuts are employed quite often in Italian swordsmanship, with some Masters (like Alfieri) using them more than others. The three most useful cuts in Italian rapier are:

- The *mandritto fendente,* a descending true-edge cut you deliver from the right to the left, almost vertically, to the opponent's head
- The *riverso fendente,* a descending true-edge cut you deliver from the left to the right, almost vertically, to the opponent's head
- The *riverso to the leg,* an oblique true-edge cut you deliver from the left to the right to the opponent's right calf.

Another cut mentioned by Capoferro is the *stramazzone,* which is a fendente-like cut delivered from the wrist.

Cuts employ a simultaneous percussive and slicing motion involving the length of the debole, and they should be strong and smartly-delivered. To the average rapier student, I recommend delivering them from the elbow; to stronger students, from the wrist.

Targets in Italian rapier – For the thrust, the main targets are the chest, the flank and the face. For the cut, they are the head and the limbs. Cuts to the body or thrusts to the limbs are consistently rare in 1500–1600 Italian swordsmanship. In this, Capoferro is the exception when he advocates a thrust to the hand. With sword and dagger, the shoulders also become targets for the thrust.

Measure – This is the distance between you and the opponent. *In measure*: a distance from which you can reach the opponent with a lunging thrust. *Out of measure*: a distance from which you cannot reach the opponent even with a lunging thrust. *Within measure*: a distance shorter than when you are in measure. This is one of the less-than-clear distinctions that Capoferro makes, compared to other authors; but if you start from these premises, understanding his words will be easier.

Tempo – Stripped of its illustrious philosophical pedigree,[17] a *tempo* (Italian for "time") is nothing but an opportune moment to strike the opponent according to the rules of the art, or at least to safely gain an advantage over him. Or, as Capoferro also says, it is the mere temporal measurement of any fencing action or motion.

Numbers of tempi are often referred to in the context of defense and riposte. If, when attacked, you parry and counterthrust in a single motion, you perform an action in one tempo (or single tempo). When you perform two distinct motions—one for the defense (simple parry), one for the riposte—you perform a two-tempi action.

Note: Capoferro calls "riposte" (*risposta*) both the counterthrust in single tempo and the riposte after a simple parry in a two-tempi action.

---

[17] In the Renaissance, the notions of *tempo* were derived primarily from Aristotle's *Physics*: tempo (time) was defined as the measurement of motion between two instances of stillness, or of stillness between two motions.

Full-intent actions and feints – A full-intent action is a simple attack designed to strike the opponent directly, without a feint. For instance, after gaining his sword, a full-intent action would be a straight thrust gliding along his blade (glide); or after he gains your sword, a full-intent action would be a cavazione. A feint is a compound attack whose first motion (the feint proper) is designed to provoke a parry, and whose subsequent motion (the cavazione) is designed to defeat the parry and to strike. As an attack, a feint cannot exist without a cavazione.

To execute a feint correctly, extend your arm and the sword-point smartly towards the target, as if performing the initial motion of a lunging thrust. As the opponent motions to parry, perform the cavazione and complete your lunging thrust on the new line.

Invitations – An invitation is when you create a deliberate opening for the opponent to attack. When he does so, you defeat him with a well-planned counter. Every time you move your sword away from the ideal line that goes from your chest to the opponent's, you are de facto performing an invitation.

How to start an action – In Italian rapier, most actions are started in one of three ways:

- By gaining the opponent's sword, then
    - Defeating his cavazione or
    - Performing a full-intent thrust by gliding along his blade (glide)
    - Performing a feint by glide
- By presenting the point in line so he gains or attempts to gain your sword, then
    - Performing a full-intent cavazione or
    - Performing a feint by cavazione
- By performing an invitation, then
    - Defeating his attack in various ways

Exceptions include taking the tempo from the opponent's motion, performing beats and other actions on the blade, performing feints without first gaining the opponent's blade, etc.

I don't want this section to become a miniature rapier treatise of its own, since I only wish to present the very basics and the concepts Capoferro skips or does not describe in much depth. Most other concepts and actions can be understood by reading Capoferro's text. I have used footnotes to explain terms that appear throughout the book, so as to make it easier to follow the Master's words, and added a glossary of common rapier fencing terms at the end of the book.

Additional Resources

To obtain additional information on principles found in Capoferro, please consider the following resources:

- Tom Leoni, *Venetian Rapier: The School, or Salle. Nicoletto Giganti's 1606 rapier fencing curriculum*, Freelance Academy Press, 2010
- The Order of the Seven Hearts' website and forum: www.salvatorfabris.com
- The Sword Forum International: www.swordforum.com
- Guy Windsor's book *The Duellist's Companion*, which is a practical training guide to his interpretation of *Gran Simulacro*
- Historical fencing symposia held internationally (such as VISS, WMAW, ISMAC, NHSC, ARMA gatherings, and others)

Great Representation *of the* Art *and* Practice *of* Fencing

Ridolfo Capoferro

1610

Translated by

TOM LEONI

To the Most Serene Lord Don Francesco Maria Feltrio della Rovere,[18] Sixth Duke of Urbino.

Every father (most serene lord the Duke), wishing to create a good name for his sons, recommends them for a position in some patrician court and attempts to secure them the noblest protection he can obtain. Similarly, finding myself with this book on fencing instruction—a book born from the best part of me—I recommend it for a place in court. The children of our intellect being the dearest ones of all, I beseech Your Excellency to find my book a position in your court, a court that is a perfect summation of a world considered perfect, as it displays within it all that is fair and good in the world itself. I dedicate this book to your son, the most serene DON FEDERICO, and I consign it to your protection. Although a child still in his infancy, who enjoys jesting and laughing, he seems to hold in his hands triumphs and spoils of war, like a new Alcides,[19] whose tender young hand, not yet equal to his wishes, threatens the Hydra and slays the serpents. His appearance reveals a generous glow, behind which shine the greatness of his ancestors, their magnanimity, valor, and the innumerable other virtues that have exhausted the pens of the greatest and most famous historians, and that will make his name illustrious beyond that of any other prince.

Indeed, to that preeminence would suffice Your Excellency's virtues, so great in number and quality to make it possible to describe you as a diligent imitator of the perfection of God.

---

18 Francesco Maria II Della Rovere (1549–1631) was the last Duke of Urbino and a famed *condottiero*, who, among other notable engagements, participated in the battle of Lepanto (1571). He produced only one male heir, Federico, to whom he bequeathed the Duchy in 1621, and to whom Capoferro dedicated this book. But upon Federico's precocious death in 1623, a broken-hearted Francesco relinquished the right to all his lands to the Papal State, thereby ending his illustrious dynasty, as well as the Duchy of Urbino.

19 The poetic patronymic for Hercules, who, according to Greek lore, overcame a great number of mythical beasts throughout his life.

I therefore beg Your Excellency not to marvel at my desire to introduce this book to your most serene house, and to recommend it to the protection of the most serene PRINCE your son; rather, acknowledging the strength of a father's love, I hope you will pardon my enthusiasm.

On my part, having considered the singular goodness that distinguishes Your Excellency and your most noble blood, I cannot fail to hope that Your Excellencies, without regard for the humility of the subject, will favor my work with their most influential favor. But even if it were not proper for your Highness to bestow so much grace on such a lowly work, let me humbly beseech you to let it rest in the common hall of your Noble Palace, and in other public places in your ample dominions. Even the mere presence among those who have the privilege of being humbly dedicated to serve and honor you will give it much glory. I pray our Lord God to keep Your Most Serene Excellencies in complete and perpetual happiness.

Siena, April 8, 1610. Of Your Serene Excellency,
The most humble and devoted servant,
Ridolfo Capoferro from Cagli

To the Kind Reader

RIDOLFO CAPO F. FROM CAGLI

It is not my intention to patronize you with pompous and high-sounding words, as I recommend to you the exercise of arms, which is my profession. Being elevated to its proper rank by its own merits, she bestows value and honor on herself. Still, she receives praise and esteem from the greatness and valor of those who righteously carry a sword at their side. Among them shines the most illustrious Signor SILVIO Piccolomini,[20] Grand Prior of the Religion of the Knights of St. Stephen in Pisa, as well as Artillery General and Master Chamberlain to His Excellency. He is not only in full possession (and with what marvelous advantages!) of this art of the sword, but also of every other chivalric art, as his heroic actions, the wonders of everyone's eyes, can attest.

But going back to the sword, she is a weapon nobler than any other, and her handling honorably entails the major part of the study of the art of arms. Therefore, I believe not only that the mere carrying of arms is not sufficient for and does not speak of the essential difference between a perfectly gallant man and a vile coward; but also, that you cannot say you can employ the sword with valor in legitimate self defense of your person and your country—you cannot say you do this honorably, unless you first humble yourself and submit yourself to the laws and rules of the art of fencing. Like a whetstone, the art of fencing makes valor finer and subtler until it reduces it to the apex of its true perfection.

This discipline is so admirable and praiseworthy that listing all its virtues would be not only redundant, but a waste of effort. I therefore do not think I can be rebuked for reducing it to a number of brief, infallible, and well-ordered rules, avoiding (as much as possible) blind and obscure confusion, deceptive and misleading uncertainty, and futile and overly-ambitious prolixity.

Now, I am aware of my weaknesses, and I do not presume that the quality of this work will match the fervor of my most-ardent enthusiasm; likewise, I am reassured that my honest and well-intentioned effort will not be totally in vain, and in that regard, I refer myself to the comparison with those who wrote on the same subject before me. Comforted therefore by the virtue of Him from whose favor we receive all our graces, I sincerely hope that my teachings—more trustworthy than showy—will bring you at least as much value and pleasure as they may bring me the smallest particle of that sweetest of tastes, true glory, which grateful souls always kindly offer to him who, with sincerity of heart, busies himself in honorably serving them.

20 A member of a notable Italian noble dynasty associated with the city of Siena from the mid-1200s. Among the famous personages it produced are popes Pius II and Pius III.

General Table of the Art of Fencing

CHAPTER I.
Of Fencing in General

1 There is nothing in this world that Nature, teacher and mother of the Universe, attends to with more skill and more concern than self-preservation. And since man is far nobler than any other creature, Nature took a most tender interest in his safety by providing him with the hand, a singular privilege that allows him to obtain anything necessary for his life. The hand also serves man to hold the sword, that most noble instrument with which man guards and protects himself against any forcible attack from an enemy—but always within the straight path of true valor and of the art of fencing.

2 From this, we can clearly discern how necessary, useful and honorable our discipline is to man. And while it is appropriate and fitting for everyone, it is most so for those who, armed with uncommon valor, embark upon the noble profession of soldiery; to these men, our art is a sort of alternative or ancillary discipline, just like a part is subject to the whole, or like an intermediate end is subordinated to the final end.

3 The goal of fencing is self-defense, from which our discipline also derives its name. In fact, fencing means to defend—fence and defense having the same connotation. This should give us an idea of the worth and the value of this discipline, a discipline that should be as dear to us as our own life and the safety of our Fatherland when we are compelled to lovingly and gallantly sacrifice our lives to its service.

4 From this, we can also see how the defense is the principal action in fencing, and that offensive actions should never be performed unless they take place in legitimate self-defense.

5 The efficient causes[21] of this discipline are four: reason, nature, art and practice. Reason puts order in nature; nature is the active virtue; art is the rule and the groomer of nature; exercise is the minister of the art.

6 Reason puts order in nature and readies the human body to fencing and to self-defense. Reason comprises judgment and will. Judgment discerns and understands what to do in order to defend; will pushes and stimulates us towards self-preservation.

7 The body obeys the orders of reason as a good servant. The body should have a normal stature and a lively eye; the legs, torso, and arms should be supple, strong and quick.

8 Reason organizes and prepares the raw material, and shapes it enough to ready it for its final form and for the perfection of the art.

9 Art regulates nature, and it guides us as a safer escort along the road of infallible truth; through the order of its instructions, it leads us to the true knowledge of self-defense.

10 Practice preserves, enhances, and establishes the strength that nature gave us for the art. Besides knowledge, it bestows us with prudence and many other virtues.

11 Art beholds nature and sees that not all she wants to do is possible due to the imperfection of matter. So she examines matter's several virtues and flaws and, like an architect, uses them to build a fine model. By doing so, art refines and polishes what is rough in nature, bringing it slowly and gradually to the utmost perfection.

12 In self-defense, art borrowed from nature the ordinary stance, the terza guard as a defensive posture and the seconda and quarta as offensive actions; it also borrowed tempo and measure, as well as the situation of the body with the weight now on the left leg (for the defense), now pushed forward onto the right leg (for the offense).

---

21 An *efficient cause* is what sets in motion the process that produces (or may produce) a result. To learn more about the causal theory alluded to here by Capoferro, please refer to Aristotle's *Metaphysics*, especially Book V.

13 Without a doubt, the earliest form of offense was boxing, in which the ordinary stance is commonly used. The terza, seconda and quarta are also seen in that discipline, as well as the fact that many know how to box in good tempo and measure.

14 Against boxing, art no doubt found the club or staff, and when this too became insufficient, it found iron. I believe that man gradually created a plethora of iron weapons of increasing quality to reflect the development of new forms of defense, until eventually man invented the sword—a weapon that is both perfect and proportional to the proper distance from which mortals naturally defend themselves.

15 Weapons exceeding the proper distance of natural defense and offense are awkward to use, and their employ should be repugnant to a civil society. Conversely, weapons that are too short are treacherous and dangerous; this is why in all Republics founded on the justice of good laws and traditions, carrying such weapons is forbidden to prevent treachery and casual murder. As a matter of fact, in the old Roman Republic (the shining ideal of a good government), the use of all weapons was forbidden, and nobody regardless of class or status could carry a sword or other arm except in war; and those found with weapons in time of peace were tried as if they were murderers.

16 Once returned home, Roman soldiers divested themselves of their weapons and replaced the short martial tunic with its longer civilian counterpart; then, they would devote their time to study and to the peacetime arts. As Sallust writes,[22] no Roman citizen exercised his body only and not his mind. So, besides the arts of war, everyone applied himself also to a peacetime duty, since the desire for peace was what made the hardships of war tolerable. Also, the end of a war would spell the end of the ideas of Captain, soldier or military pay.

17 Nowadays, soldiers represent a greater burden (to princes, lords and especially the people) in peacetime rather than wartime. Since they are not versed in any other occupation besides war, they hate peace, often becoming the architects of wickedness and unrest.

18 Going back to our subject, the sword is a most useful and perfect weapon, since it is proportional to the distance from which offense is normally performed. The more a weapon differs from the distance of natural defense and offense, the more it is inhuman and contrary to nature, thereby becoming useless in a civil society. There is only one road to virtue and reason: although hard and rocky, it is the road from which nature never departs. Instead, the road to error and ignorance can be traveled quickly by slipping and sliding through many paths. Similarly, there is only one straight line, a line that can only be observed by the true artist; instead, the oblique lines are infinite, and can be observed by everyone. This is why, in our times, the offenses and defenses are being multiplied without end. Arts and human industry initially imitate nature, and as long as they follow in her footsteps, they are beneficial to our species; but as soon as they depart from nature's path, they start going against their initial nobility, they fall in the traps of harmful curiosity and eventually throw humanity into the abyss of ignorance, taking him from the Golden Age into filthy muck.

19 Up to this point, we have discussed the powers of nature, art, and practice as the efficient causes of defense. From these proceed all the advantages and disadvantages in swordplay, although the main factors in this regard are the just stature of a person and the proper length of the sword. A tall man who uses a sword proportional to his body will undoubtedly be the first to arrive into measure. In light of this, I seem to recall that in certain countries it is forbidden to manufacture a sword-blade longer than another, to compensate for the natural disadvantage of those shorter in stature. On one hand, it does not appear fair that a fencer favored by nature should also be able to enjoy the advantages of the art, since the former advantage should be sufficient. On the other, however, the advantage given to him by

[22] Sallust was a Roman historian (86–35 BC). In his work *De Bello Catilinario*, VIII, he wrote: "ingenium nemo sine corpore exercebat" (nobody exercised the mind without the body).

nature would be unfairly taken away from him by giving him a sword proportionally shorter than that of a smaller man with whom he should fight. The smaller man, in turn, could have other advantages given to him by art and practice—advantages that could more than offset the natural factors. In such specific cases, human prudence is insufficient to provide remedies.

20 The art of fencing is very ancient. It was invented at the time of Ninus, king of the Assyrians, who became ruler and master of the world by virtue of his martial proficiency. Along with monarchy, the appreciation for this art was passed to the Persians; through the valor of Cyrus, it arrived to Macedonia, then to Greece and finally to Rome. As Vegetius witnesses, Romans took to the field their fencing masters, whom they called *Campi ductores, vel doctores,* which means guides, or masters of the field. These masters taught soldiers how to perform thrusting and cutting attacks against a post. Like the Romans, today we Italians carry the torch of fencing, although we do so more in the salle than on the battlefield, since in our times wars are conducted more through artillery and musketry than through the sword, whose role is limited to the ceremony of victory.

21 If we take the word "science" in its strict meaning, our discipline is an art, not a science, because fencing does not consist of examining eternal and divine things going beyond the will of humans. Instead, it is an active art (as opposed to a craft or manual art), and a close ministry of civilian science. It is such because its creations disappear as soon as they are performed, just as is the case with virtue; and performance of our art does not leave a tangible artifact or object as do the mechanical or popular arts—which our discipline greatly surpasses, although some of them are celebrated as noble.

22 The substance of fencing is composed of the rules on how to defend with the sword; its form consists in the order and truth of its rules, which are always correct and infallible.

23 It is now time to gather all that we have briefly examined so far, and to establish the foundation of our discipline, which is the correct and proper definition of fencing according to the rules. From there, we will then address the remainder of the art's principles.

CHAPTER II.
The Definition of Fencing, and Its Explanation

24 Fencing is the art of skillfully defending oneself with the sword.

25 It is an art because it is a collection of rules that are perpetually valid, well-ordered, and useful to a civil society.

26 Truth is what establishes the correct order of the rules of fencing. It should not be assessed through the ignorance of some teachers and authors who have years of experience but no real knowledge; these men make substance out of shadows, mix apples and oranges, and jump from one subject to another without connection. Truth should instead be assessed on its own merits, according to the validity of its nature.

27 The usefulness of these rules is clear, because they teach a natural, just, and honest defense. It is impossible to doubt what great utility this defense brings to our lives, since we can see every day what are the fruits of its use. Since the sword is a weapon devised to defend in proper measure—from which either fencer can naturally strike—we often see that both contenders attend to the defense and rarely attack (the attack being the last remedy to save one's life). This would not happen if weapons were out of proportion, i.e., greater or smaller than what is required by natural defense.

28 The object that separates fencing from the other forms of knowledge is effective defense with the sword.

CHAPTER III.
The Part of Fencing Consisting in the Knowledge of the Sword

29 The parts of fencing are two: the knowledge of the sword and the handling of the sword. The knowledge of the sword is the first part of fencing, and it teaches us to be familiar with the sword so that we can make good use of it.

30 The sword is a sharp metal weapon, designed for defense at a distance from which either fencer can naturally strike, exposing his life to danger.

31 The substance of which the sword is made is iron. Iron is a defensive substance, undoubtedly found to be better than wood to easily fend off the harm that men inflict daily on one-another.

32 The exterior form of the sword is sharply pointed; if it was not pointed, it could not be used to keep the opponent in the distance of natural offense.

33 The purpose of the sword is the defense, which means chiefly keeping the opponent sufficiently far to prevent him from striking. This type of defense is very natural, since it can be effected without harming a fellow human. I have heard a man of letters state that "defending" in Latin means fending off or avoiding something that could harm us if we allowed it to get too close.

34 The other meaning of defending is offending and striking, which is the last subsidiary remedy[23] of defense. Offense is to be used if the opponent exceeds the initial boundaries of the defense, and gets so close that I would be in danger of being struck if I did not act first. When the opponent crosses beyond the boundaries of the defense to enter those of the offense, in fact, I am no longer obligated to exercise any regard for his safety. This is true if he comes against me carrying a weapon with the intent of harming me—naturally, from a distance sufficient for him to reach me.

35 The length of the sword depends on its purpose, which is to defend from the distance just described.

36 Therefore, the sword should be twice as long as the arm, or as long as the extended step.[24] This length is also the same as that between the sole of my foot and just under the armpit.

37 The parts of the sword are two: the forte and the debole. The forte starts at the hilt and ends at mid-blade; the debole is the remainder of the blade. The role of the forte is to parry, that of the debole is to strike.

38 The edges are true and false. The true edge is that facing the ground when the hand is in the natural position. As the hand is turned to the inside or outside of its natural situation, it produces the false edge. The first position mentioned here (that of the true edge) is that of the terza, which is the position of the sword while in guard; the others are positions of the sword not used while in guard, but while striking.

39 I only divide the debole into true and false edge, and not the forte, because what I just said does not apply to the forte, its role being purely defensive. Therefore, if the forte did not have an edge and was bated instead of sharp, it would not be a disadvantage at all. The hilt serves not only to grip the sword, but also to cover your body and especially your head while you strike.

---

23 A *subsidiary remedy* (remedium subsidiarium) is a concept in jurisprudence by which a course of action is resorted to after exhausting the alternatives.

24 This is the distance between the feet in the position of a fencing lunge (see plate 5). For an explanation of technical concepts, please refer to the glossary or to the section "What You Need to Know to Tackle Capoferro."

CHAPTER IV.
Measure

40 Up to this point, we have discussed the first part of fencing, which consists in the knowledge of the sword; now, we will begin presenting the second part, which is the handling of our weapon.

41 The handling of the sword is the second part of fencing. It teaches us how to handle the sword, namely how to get ready for the defense and how to execute the defense itself. Preparing the defense is the first part of the handling of the sword, since it is when the combatants are set in the appropriate distance and in a posture suitable for defending in tempo. This part is subdivided into two sections: in the first, we will discuss measure and tempo.

42 In the second, we will discuss the positioning of the various parts of the body.

43 Measure is usually defined as a distance between one point and another. For example, in the art of fencing, measure is the distance between the point of my sword and the torso of my opponent: this distance can be wide or narrow. Then, some unit of measure is usually adopted to measure distance; in the practice of fencing, this is usually the natural arm, which is employed to measure all distances. In the practice of our art, the natural arm has all the qualities and the prerequisites of a regular unit of measure.

44 Measure is that proper distance between the point of my sword and the opponent's torso from which I can strike him. Every action I make with the sword, including the defense, should be effected according to this distance.

45 Narrow measure can either be of the foot or of the extended arm. The measure of the foot can either be firm-footed or with an accrescimento.[25]

46 Wide measure is that distance from which I can strike the opponent by performing an accrescimento with the right foot; and this is the first narrow measure.[26]

47 The firm-footed narrow measure is that distance from which I can strike the opponent by merely bending my torso and legs forward.

48 The narrowest measure happens when, from the wide measure, I can strike the opponent in the arm that he holds extended and uncovered; this may be his dagger-arm or his sword-arm. Such action should be performed while moving the left foot back, and the strike should be accompanied by the right foot.

49 The first (wide) measure is worth one tempo and a half; the second is worth one tempo, the third a half tempo. This is according to the three distances which, depending on their scale, call for different amounts of time. What I presented above should suffice concerning measure; we will now speak of the theory of tempo.[27]

---

25 A step forward of the front foot, as also happens in a fencing lunge

26 See note in the introductory chapter "Capoferro, His Treatise and Its Importance to the Modern Student."

27 The first... the second... the third...: wide, narrow and narrowest measures. Also, please refer to next chapter, paragraph 51.

CHAPTER V.
Tempo

50 In fencing, the word *tempo* means three things. Firstly, it means that proper interval of motion or stillness I require to carry out a specific action; in this case, it does not matter if the time is long or short, the only concern being that I carry out the action. In the art of fencing, I require a specific and appropriate interval of time and motion to arrive into measure; it does not matter whether I arrive sooner or later—what matters is that I arrive where I intended to arrive. Let us take this example: I move to find the measure, approaching little by little while the opponent remains still for a sufficiently long amount of time for me to arrive into measure. Although in this example it has taken me a long time to get into measure, nothing has prevented me from accomplishing my goal: I have arrived into measure in tempo, since in the time of my motion, the adversary has remained still. The time of my motion has been equal to that of my opponent's stillness; his stillness has determined the quantity of my motion. While in guard and seeking the measure, what matters is only the relation of tempo created by the combatants as they move and stop in turn until they eventually arrive in measure. This is why, in these actions, the speed of motion and the shortness of stillness are irrelevant; actually, while seeking the proper measure, it is far better to proceed (as the saying goes) with a leaden foot, with the torso kept back and with the weight of the body on the left leg and using an ordinary stance. This is a suitable posture with which to carefully and cautiously approach the proper measure.

51 Next, the word tempo is taken to mean speed in relation to the length or brevity of motion or stillness. As in the art of fencing there are three measures (or distances) from which to strike, so there are three distinct tempi. In this case, it is not enough that I reach a certain end; what also matters is that I reach it with the required speed and promptness. The wide measure with accrescimento requires a certain tempo—i.e., a given space of continuous stillness or motion of the combatants' swords or bodies—that is short but not as short as that required by the narrow measure of a firm foot. The narrowest measure requires instead an extra-quick tempo, since even the smallest motion I make with my sword and the shortest stillness of my opponent would be enough for me to reach my design while in this measure; this extra-short tempo is therefore called half-tempo. The tempo required to strike from the less narrow measure that we call narrow measure of firm foot is a whole tempo; lastly, the tempo required to strike from the wide measure (which requires an accrescimento) is a whole tempo and a half.

52 In the first kind of tempo—which is when I seek the wide measure—quickness of motion and stillness does not matter; this is why we do not measure it by half or whole tempi. This measurement of tempi is only used for strikes. This is also why the position of the body while striking is completely different from that while seeking the narrow measure: in the former case, the position is comfortable so that the measure can be gradually found; in the latter, the position is bold so that I can quickly unleash the attack.

53 Tempo is nothing but the measurement of stillness and motion. The stillness of my sword-point measures the motion of my adversary's body; the motion of my adversary's body measures the stillness of my sword-point. Now, for this tempo to be proper, the interval of time in which my opponent's body is still needs to equal the motion of my sword-point. So, let's say, for instance, that I am in the wide measure trying to gain the narrow measure, and that I move the point of my sword in order to do so; while I move, the opponent's body needs to remain still. Thus, the stillness of his body becomes the measurement of the motion of my sword-point. Instead, if I moved to strike the opponent before he ceased being still, the tempi would be unequal, and my action would bring me either no fruit or great danger. Now, let's instead suppose that we both moved to seek the measure, and we both thought we had found it: by simultaneously moving against one-another, we would cause our attacks to be unsuccessful. This is because the tempo in which we moved to strike was not proper, according to the distance we had reached. In this

example, the motion of my sword-point measures the motion of my adversary's body, and the motion of his sword-point measures the motion of my body. Also, it can frequently happen that both fencers strike one-another in contratempo after both arriving into the narrow measure in an equal tempo.

54 In the wide measure, tempo requires patience; in the narrow measure, it requires speed both in striking and in recovering.

55 Tempo in the narrow measure can be missed either through one's natural shortcomings or through faulty technique and insufficient practice.

56 These natural shortcomings consist in slowness of the legs, arms, or body; this, in turn, comes from either weakness or excessive body-weight (as is the case with men who are too fat or too thin).

57 Faulty technique consists in failing to seek the narrow measure properly, which should be with the torso leaning over the left leg, in the ordinary stance and with the right arm extended. All these elements must move in concert in order to produce a joint result, and they also need to move in a proper distance. Instead, if the point of the sword is very advanced while the leg is too far behind—or if the leg is too far ahead while the arm is behind—the sword will not be carried with the necessary promptness, exactness, and speed. For this reason, those who seek the measure with a less-than-proportionate distance between limbs may indeed get there, but they will never be in tempo to strike, since they will lack the most favorable timing of the narrow measure, which is given by promptness, exactness and speed.

58 Insufficient practice causes loss of tempo either because the body still lacks the necessary suppleness, or because of the acquisition of bad habits such as indulging in futile feints, cavazioni, controcavazioni, and similar.

59 From what we have just seen, we can clearly note that it is wrong to say, as many do, that tempo can only be taken from the motion of the opponent's body or sword. Instead, tempo is a function of my and the opponent's motion as well as our stillness. In other words, tempo is not just a measure of motion, but rather of motion and stillness.

60 Closing the subject of tempo, every motion and every stillness (mine and the opponent's) together form a tempo—since they measure one-another.

CHAPTER VI.
The Body, Beginning with the Head

61 In our discipline, the head is truly important, since when it is properly situated, it can assess measures and tempi. Therefore, you need to carry it so that it can act as a sentry and command the field on all sides.

62 The correct placement of the head while in guard and seeking the measure is in a straight line with the sword, so that the eyes can catch every stillness and motion of the opponent's sword and body, and immediately spot where to strike and where to defend. Placing the head in this manner enables your eyes to cast their visual rays in a straight line, which would not be the case if you were to hold it higher or lower; when unable to cast your rays on all sides, you cannot easily assess a tempo or break away from one.[28]

63 While standing in guard and seeking the measure, the head should lean towards the left shoulder, whereas while striking it should lean towards the right shoulder.

64 While standing in guard and seeking the measure, the head should be kept back as much as possible, whereas while striking it should be extended forward as much as possible.

[28] *Break away from one*: escape an opponent's attack or his gaining an advantage over you.

65 While striking, the head should lean somewhat to one side, depending on whether you are inside or outside; in this manner, it will remain covered by the hilt and the sword-arm.

66 There are other motions of the head that are sometimes performed while passing, retreating or voiding in a variety of guards and attacks; but these cannot be considered acceptable, since they all involve leaving the straight line. I define the straight line as the line that divides my body and the opponent's in two at the flank. Conversely, I call oblique that line that starts at my body (or the opponent's) and goes on either side. The whole game of fencing should be assessed according to this rule.

CHAPTER VII.
The Body

67 While standing in guard and seeking the measure, the body should be bent, that is, leaning back so as to form a barely-discernible angle with the right thigh and an obtuse angle with the left. The left shoulder should be on the same perpendicular line as the left foot, and the right shoulder should be situated exactly above the middle of your stance while in guard.

68 While striking, the body should be pushed forward, so that the right thigh forms an obtuse angle with the body, and the point of the right shoulder is on the same perpendicular line as your right toes. The left thigh and leg should be extended forward in an oblique line, so that the left shoulder is above the mid-point of your offensive stance.

69 When striking, the body should be extended forward in a straight line. Depending on whether the strike is to the outside or the inside, the body will slightly lean to either side, but always remaining very close to the straight line.

70 The reasons why the body should be bent as described are the following. Firstly, this makes it easier to keep one's openings farther away, better covered and more defended—since the farther the target, the harder to hit. Secondly, by doing so, attacks have more reach and are quicker and stronger—since the farther away attacks come from, the safer and better they are.

71 Besides the bending of the body and its posture while in guard, seeking the measure or striking, there is also the consideration of voiding, which diminishes the body's width and (as the body bends) reduces its height.

72 Voiding should be done in such way that only half of the chest is visible to the opponent, not only while in guard and seeking the measure, but also while striking. The less of your chest you uncover, the easier to advance and strike in a straight line, while the more chest you uncover, the more you lose measure and tempo.

73 There are those who are fond of guards, counter-guards, gaining the sword on either side, above and below, and those who like feints and counter-feints, oblique steps, voiding steps, and crossed steps. Such fencers usually position and move their bodies in many bizarre ways—all things done randomly outside of any solid and valid principle; therefore, we will gladly leave these actions to the men who invented them.

CHAPTER VIII.
The Arms

74 While in guard and seeking the measure, your right arm should be somewhat bent. The upper part of the arm should slope downwards just enough to allow the elbow to be exactly in front of your flank and to be on a perpendicular line with the right knee. The slightly-withdrawn forearm should form a straight line with the sword.

75 While standing in guard and seeking the measure, the left arm, thigh, and leg should provide a counterweight to the body, the right thigh, and the right leg. The upper part of the left arm should be extended so that it is in line with the left knee; the elbow should be opposite the left flank, and the forearm should be kept somewhat gathered, so that its extension can help push the body forward while striking (which would not be possible if the left forearm was kept loose).

76 While striking, the right arm should be extended in a straight line, with the lower side of the arm and the hand turning upward—to the inside or outside, depending on which side the strike occurs.[29]

77 While striking, the left arm should be extended so as to form a straight line with the right arm, and should be turned according to whether the strike is inside or outside. If it were carried only a little farther forward or if it stopped in an oblique line, it would cause the measure to be diminished and the tempo to be slower.

78 The sword should be regarded as one with the arm, forming a straight line with the forearm just in front of the bend of your right flank. While standing in guard and seeking the measure, this straight line should divide the body in equal halves both vertically and horizontally. This is because, by corresponding exactly with the flank, the sword remains always ready to defend any part of the body that may be attacked—since the distance between the head and the flank is the same as that between the flank and the knee. There is no need to worry about the legs, since in the wide measure of the extended step they cannot be attacked without the opponent coming so far forward with his body that he incurs considerable danger.

79 The location and positioning of the sword while striking are the same as those of the arm. The false edge should be turned upwards, depending on whether the strike is inside or outside.

80 Please take notice that the point of your sword always remains aimed at the opponent's openings (the right flank and thigh). Do not deviate from this rule, as targeting the left side is wrong in terms of measure and tempo, since the left side may be removed from danger very quickly. This is not the case with the right side, which is necessarily exposed.

81 It is not advisable to stand in guard with the arm withdrawn. With a withdrawn arm, I cannot easily assess the measure in which I stand; then, I will have problems seeking the measure, since my sword-point is too far from the opponent's body. With a withdrawn arm, it is impossible to take the right measure, to strike in tempo or to keep the opponent away from the proper distance from which he can strike me. Therefore, a withdrawn arm does not suit the purpose for which the sword was invented. Likewise, it does not suit the offense: how can I strike from the measure of the extended step, if by keeping the sword-point so far from the opponent, I cannot even take that measure correctly? And the measure of the extended step is much better than the narrow measures, since it is preferable to strike the opponent from farther away rather than from nearby. Moreover, keeping the arm withdrawn is not good for shooting out a powerful thrust,[30] which is done by pushing the arm and the body forward. It is the extension of the body and the foot that lengthens the measure, not the extension of the arm. The forward leg and the body push the sword-arm forward, but rest on the left leg. In other words, the whole body-weight as well as the right leg rest on the left leg. So, when the left leg shoots the thrust, it propels the body forward; the right thigh ends above the right shin, at which point the latter becomes the bearer of the whole body-weight after this comes forward propelled by the thrust.

29 Turning upward: as you strike, your hand will usually turn from terza to quarta or seconda, thus causing the true edge of the sword to turn "upward" from facing down to facing to either side. See also paragraph 79.

30 Here and elsewhere, "shooting the thrust": powerful and vivid informal expression used by Capoferro, which I have translated literally from his *sparare la botta*.

82 A completely extended arm while in guard is also something I cannot advise, since it keeps the sword out of its correct placement from where I can defend my body and strike the opponent with ease. Also, it is not ideal to aid the body in shooting the thrust, which will as a result be less vigorous. All other postures and movements of the arm are outside of the scope of fencing and striking in a straight line.

CHAPTER IX.
The Thighs, the Legs, the Feet, and the Stance

83 While standing in guard and seeking the narrow measure, the right leg, thigh, and foot are directed straight forward; the leg should form an oblique line, leaning back at a slant. The left leg, thigh, and foot are instead directed to the left side, with the knee as bent as possible; the inside of the left heel should be in line with the point of the right heel.

84 While striking, the right knee should bend as much as possible, so that the leg and the thigh form a very acute angle; conversely, the left leg and thigh should be extended forward at a slant in an oblique line.

85 The stance is defined as a suitable distance between the legs, both while I am still and while I move. It should be ideal for standing in guard while seeking the measure and for striking. Depending on its size, we have the fully narrow stance, the half-stance, the regular or ordinary stance and the extraordinary stance.

86 In the practice of fencing, I only approve of the ordinary stance, in which the body can stand in guard comfortably and steadily, and which is conducive for seeking the narrow measure just by a small extension of the stance. Conversely, standing in guard with a narrower stance would make the fencer's base too narrow and weak, and would be insufficient to hold the body-weight. Also, a narrower stance would lead gradually to a disordering of the stance; if the measure was sought with steps and half-steps, tempo would be lost and the attack could not be delivered with the necessary speed. Although such stances may be good at times, they are only useful out of measure—for walking, getting or recovering in guard.

87 In order to be clearer, we will call the fencing stance the "martial" or "soldierly" stance. This can either be ordinary or extraordinary. The ordinary is used to stand in guard and seek the narrow measure; the extraordinary is formed with an accrescimento of the front foot while striking.

88 The moving steps can be classified in many ways—forward, backward, sideways, and oblique, the latter with or without crossing the feet; also, it is possible to step with one foot or with both. Legs can be moved to perform a whole step, to make a whole step smaller or to retreat or perform a void.

89 In my opinion, there are only two main ways for the legs to stand and move. The first is used while standing in guard to seek the narrow measure or to break measure; the second is used for striking.

90 I really don't know what else stepping sideways is good for except showing off, displaying bravery or perhaps assessing the opponent's strengths. When faced with an opponent who uses this kind of stepping while in guard, you can make use of all the narrow and regular stances, although even in this situation I think the regular stance is best.

91 There are some who use lateral steps when the opponent stands in guard with the sword at an oblique line, in order to gain his blade to the outside. But even here, I think that it would be better to seek the narrow measure in a straight line rather than proceeding outside of the proper rule. Some fencers also use the lateral step as a voiding action in response to the opponent's attack—meeting him in quarta or seconda or to the outside or inside (as the occasion requires). However, the opponent could also be met in quarta or seconda in a straight line (observing the tempo and the measure) rather than by stepping out laterally.

92 Crossing the left foot behind your right while performing an inquartata is a useless and unnecessary action. It constrains the body and it shortens the motion of the right arm as it strikes, resulting in loss of tempo. Likewise, voiding with the right leg to the opponent's left while performing an inquartata is also pointless, and is better used in a friendly match than in a real fight or in a duel.

93 Passing steps are not advisable, because they cause loss of measure and tempo. While your left leg moves forward, the body, the right leg, and the sword-arm cannot do so with the necessary speed or without getting you in danger of a riposte.

94 Recovering is especially necessary after striking: as I strike, I necessarily uncover my body—therefore if I wait too long I can easily receive the opponent's riposte.

CHAPTER X.
The Defense, the Guard

95 Up to this point, we have examined the first part of the handling of the sword: we learned the correct distance and the appropriate position of each part of the body necessary for the defense. Now, we will move on to the defense itself.

96 The defense is the second part of the handling of the sword, which is where we learn how to make use of the sword to defend ourselves. In turn, it is composed of two parts—a defensive one (or guard, as we may call it) and an offensive one.

97 The guard is the position of the arm and the sword extended in a straight line right in the middle of the parts that can be attacked; the body is well situated in an ordinary step to keep the opponent far from where he can attack, while being able to attack him in case he comes dangerously close.

98 Only the terza, therefore, can be classified as a guard—not with the hilt to the outside of the knee, but situated so as to divide the torso in two halves; not high, not low, but right in the middle of the parts of the body that are necessarily open, so as to be equidistant to them and equally ready for all the attacks and defenses.

99 The prima and the seconda are not guards, because they are not adequate for seeking the measure: they leave the body too uncovered and they are not equidistant to all the parts of the body to be attacked or defended.[31] The quarta also leaves the body too uncovered, and it is more a striking position than a defensive one.

100 There are three reasons why it is difficult to strike the intended target. One is the distance to the target. Another is the fact that the target may be covered so as to be barely visible beyond what defends it. The third is that even when the target is uncovered, as soon as the danger of the strike gets near it, it gets quickly covered.

101 Our guard encompasses all these benefits. It maintains the target far away and keeps it as refused as possible by virtue of the bending and the profiling of the body. Also, it easily covers those parts of the body that have to be left exposed, and it is ready to defend them by virtue of being equidistant to all of them. Lastly, it is conducive to walking securely and taking the tempo and measure, which is the ultimate perfection of the guard.

---

31 This is a point specifically contested by Alfieri in his 1640 work *La Scherma*. In Chapter VIII, he states "Capoferro [...] vilifies the prima and the seconda to the point of stating that they are not guards. This opinion is badly conceived. These are indeed guards, although they may not be as perfect as the others."

102 I will not even mention changing from one guard to another, since there is only one guard that I consider good.

103 The offense is a form of defense in which I seek the measure and attack my opponent.

CHAPTER XI.
How to Seek the Measure

104 The offense consists of two parts: seeking the measure and striking.

105 Seeking the measure is a form of offense in which, while in guard, I try to arrive in the narrow measure so I can strike.

106 There are three ways to seek the measure. One is when I move to seek the measure and the opponent remains stationary; one is when I remain stationary and the opponent moves; the other is when both I and the opponent move.

107 The tempo of this action needs to be accurate; it must be proportional to the last boundary of the wide measure—which is where the tempo for seeking the measure expires, giving way to the tempo of another action: striking.

108 In order for this tempo to be accurate, you need to exercise patience until you are in the aforementioned distance; do not move to strike before then.

109 Here is an example. I stand in guard and seek the measure while the opponent is already in an offensive distance. While he seeks the measure or tries to attack me, he causes his sword to advance; so I need to keep my sword-point still until the opponent arrives to the edge of the wide measure, and not perform an attack before then. In this action, his motion should measure my stillness, and my stillness his motion. If I moved prematurely before the proper amount of stillness required to allow the opponent to enter the edge of the wide measure, the tempo would be wrong; also wrong is how I would have sought the measure. This equal motion and stillness until the edge of the narrow measure is a tempo that should not be considered in relation to its speed; instead, it needs to be exactly proportional to the last boundary of the wide measure. Similarly, the end of the tempo of the wide measure is to seek the narrow measure—or the beginning of the tempo of the strike.

110 While seeking the narrow measure, many fencers perform cavazioni, controcavazioni, feints, and counter-feints, gain a span of the opponent's sword, walk sideways to all directions and twist, extend and withdraw their bodies in many extravagant ways. These actions are all outside of the correct rules, and were perhaps invented to fool the gullible and make plays difficult. As far as gaining the sword, when I absolutely have to as I am in guard seeking the measure, it is only necessary that I gain the opponent's debole with my forte in a straight line, placing my blade above his without touching it. Only when I strike should I push my forte against the opponent's debole—to the inside or outside depending on the situation.

111 Performing a cavazione is advisable, but only if the opponent has gained my sword and removed me from the straight line. In this case I can—or rather should—pull back and perform a cavazione with a little withdrawing of the body or feet, after which I should immediately replace my sword on the straight line and start seeking the measure. Cavazioni are performed against the gaining of the sword; as gaining the sword is performed by moving the sword forward, the cavazione should be performed while moving it back.

CHAPTER XII.
Of Strikes

112 Striking is the very last offensive action in fencing. Once I have arrived in the narrow measure, striking consists in extending my body, legs, and arms all in one tempo as far forward as possible in order to hit the opponent. This action can be performed either firm-footed or by performing an accrescimento—depending on the width of the narrow measure and depending on whether I find it more comfortable to take one measure or the other. If I lose the first measure because I am too slow or the opponent too fast, I can always use the second and perform a firm-footed strike. In this case, I do not need to hurry my step. I only need to bend the right knee, not to seek a closer measure by means of an accrescimento.

113 Striking can be accomplished in three ways. I may strike the opponent while I am stationary and the opponent moves either to seek the measure or to attack; I may also strike while he is stationary and I move to seek the measure; lastly, I can strike when we both move to seek the measure and attack. This is the main difference: when he moves to strike me, I must strike him firm-footed, since his motion would make it impossible for me to take the proper measure by striking with an accrescimento. This is why I need to use a narrower measure; instead, when the opponent moves to seek the measure, I can make use of the accrescimento while striking him.

114 Strikes can be performed to the inside or outside—depending on the relation between the sword and the different parts of the body. Striking to the inside is done in quarta; to the outside in seconda. Strikes may be high or low depending on the opponent's opening, which also gives me the measure from my sword-point.

115 While striking, I necessarily parry at the same time,[32] as long as I strike on the straight line and with the body in its correct position. When I do this in tempo and from the right measure, it is impossible for the opponent to hit me with a cut or a thrust, since the forte of my sword proceeds forward on the straight line, thereby covering my whole body.

116 The cut is of little importance, since it is impossible to use it in the narrow measure. The arc described by my arm and sword leaves me completely open and makes me lose measure; instead, it gives the opponent a good tempo in which to hit me. Although the cut is of some utility, the thrust can always be employed more fruitfully from the same measure and in the same tempo.

117 However, the cut is undoubtedly preferable to the thrust while on horseback. Since it is not my own legs but the horse that carries me, I am unable to seek the correct measure and tempo to push the body and the arm forward.[33] Instead, while on horseback I am freer to rotate my arm as I wish, which is the appropriate motion for delivering cuts.

---

32 Parry: in sword alone, as it is likely to be the case in this paragraph, Capoferro means performing opposition with the hilt and/or the forte of the blade. A term such as "opposition" for this principle does not occur in the Italian fencing literature I have examined until the 19th century, although the concept is often emphasized in the age of the rapier (for instance, here by Capoferro).

33 This is another point specifically contested by Alfieri (*La Scherma*, 1640) in Chapter XVIII. "Capoferro's argument [...] does not stand at all, since from the distance where I can use a cut, I can also use a thrust."

CHAPTER XIII.
The Dagger

118 This short chapter will be enough to describe how the dagger was devised for added safety in case I unleash a thrust without worrying about parrying, and the opponent decides to hit me in the most suitable opening. The dagger's best function is that of parrying a riposte. However, as we know, all medicines come with some side-effects; this is the case with the dagger, whose use makes the body more open and makes attacks a little shorter. This was the original purpose of the dagger; later, the art departed from its first objective and devised many techniques for it—as it did with the sword. Still, let's not waste any more words by saying that all these techniques are better executed with the sword.

Here Follows the Great Representation of the Practice of Fencing; Beginning with the Explanation of the Difference Between Art and Practice

There is an enormous difference between art and practice. This difference is not any slighter than that between reason and chance, confusion, and order, or between knowledge and opinion. To make this more understandable, let me explain art as I remember it defined by men of letters. Art is a collection of rules that are useful to—and well ordered for—civil society. Just as one blossom does not springtime make, a single rule, or indeed any number of rules, is not sufficient to make an art.

The only rules that make the grade are those that prove useful; the ineffectual ones or those clouded by false and deceitful opinions are instead discarded. This is why art is not governed by individual choice; rather, it is the ruling principle of truth that directs its rules. Thus, truth dictates that art should not be founded on shifting sands, and that it should only teach principles that are infallible and perpetually valid. Conversely, truth does not acknowledge rules that do not measure up to their own laws.

On the other hand, the practice of an art is a much broader subject. Besides consisting of what is true, practice also points out mistakes and many other details that may take place in different ways. In order to show the effects of all these factors, practice also borrows from other disciplines. Even in our society, we often see how one man cannot exercise his trade or his art alone without the help of his fellow citizens; likewise, arts, sciences, and professions are all interlinked and depend on one-another for their practical applications. Along the same lines, in our society every man has his separate task, home, and possessions; similarly, arts and sciences have distinct objectives and principles beyond which they may not trespass.

Teachers who fail to note this difference between art and practice usually fall into some grave pitfalls; whether their instruction is presented in a book or in a salle, they ramble and confuse matters so much that they even contradict their own words. If they began instead by building a solid foundation of rules that are infallible and well-ordered by the art, they would easily and quickly see their students progress to the degree of perfection that we all strive for in this art.

In light of these considerations, I have tried to facilitate the study of fencing by smoothing out its intricacies and by steering away from the darkness of confusion. I have instead narrowed down the art to a small number of rules distinct from its practice, while I will now present a few illustrations most of which are explanatory of our art. I will leave it to others to dedicate their study to the uncertain and unlimited details of specific and ever-changing situations, something which unfortunately happens every day in the practice of fencing. If this ever-changing variety of things needs to be taught, I think it would be better to explain it a little at a time in the school, since it cannot be taught by theory alone.

Anyway, it is now time for me to present some recommendations and ideas, to explain some terms that pertain to the practice of fencing, and to display my illustrations.

A Few Recommendations about Fencing

1 When you face your opponent, always look at his sword-hand—looking anywhere else would mislead you. When you look at his hand, you can see all its motions and rests, which enables you to use your judgment to decide what to do.

PARRYING, STRIKING, AND VOIDING

2 A good fencer should never parry without riposting; nor should he ever strike unless he is sure to parry the opponent's riposte.[34] Likewise, he should not perform a void without delivering a strike. If he needs to parry with the dagger, as he moves the dagger for the defense, he needs to move the sword for the offense.

THE BENEFITS OF SWORD ALONE

3 You should know that sword alone is the queen of all other weapon-combinations. Therefore, practicing sword alone is at least as beneficial as practicing any other weapon. With the sword alone, it is easier to learn to parry, void, perform cavazioni and controcavazioni, gain the opponent's sword in all guards, etc. When performing all these techniques, keep your arm extended, since by doing so you will push all the opponent's attacks safely out of your presence.

HOW TO ACT AGAINST A BRUTISH MAN

4 If you are faced with a brutish man who delivers one strong attack after the other without any regard for measure or tempo, this is what you should do. Firstly, make use of the play of half-tempo (which I will teach you later on): as he delivers his attacks, you can strike him in the sword-hand or sword-arm with your point or with a cut. Also, you can pull your body back, let his attack pass you by and then immediately push a thrust to his face or chest.

HOW TO BECOME A PERFECT FENCER

5 In order to become a perfect fencer, it is not enough to take lessons from a master. You must also try to measure yourself every day with a variety of fencers and, if you can, practice with those who know more than you do. Fencing with so many skilled practitioners will refine your abilities to perfection.

THE SAFEST GUARD

6 As you know, in the section on the art I have only recommended that low guard we call terza, which features the sword held horizontally, in a straight line, thereby dividing the right flank equally in the middle. The point should always be directed to the middle of the opponent's torso—that is, the part of his body nearest to you. The high guards are not as safe because they can leave you vulnerable to thrusts or to cuts to the leg, while the low guards do not present this danger. The only natural form of attack from low guards is the thrust.

---

34 As you have seen in the introductory chapter "What You Need to Know to Tackle Capoferro," Capoferro calls a "riposte" both a counterthrust in a single tempo and a riposte after a simple parry in a two-tempi action.

THE FUTILITY OF FEINTS

7 Feints are not effective, because they cause loss of tempo and measure. Also, you can only perform the feint either from out of measure or from the measure: in the first case, I don't even move; in the second, while you perform the feint, I strike you.

FROM WHOM YOU SHOULD LEARN

8 There are some who, as soon as they gain a little knowledge and experience, start teaching others. However, they teach without any real foundation or rule, since they don't understand that there is a big difference between knowing and teaching. Teaching fencing the right way requires long experience, because acquiring the precise knowledge of tempo and measure takes time. Someone who does not have the knowledge of tempo and measure cannot teach and can only become an imperfect fencer. Make sure you do not seek instruction from this kind of man.

GAINING THE SWORD

9 Knowing how to gain the opponent's sword from every guard is both useful and beautiful. However, it is also important to know how to free your sword in case the opponent gains it. When the opponent gains your sword, there are three things you need to remember. Firstly, never perform a cavazione followed by a full cut, or a cavazione followed by a parry and riposte. Secondly, you may pull back with your body and lower your sword; if the opponent follows you to gain your sword again, take the tempo from the forward motion of his right foot and strike him above or below his sword, depending on what is more suitable at the time.

Lastly, be advised that by "gaining the sword" I mean the same as "*stringere* the sword."

STRIKING IN CONTRATEMPO

10 Striking in contratempo can be done in several ways, although I only approve of two. The first is when your sword is in quarta with the point somewhat towards your right; if the opponent advances to gain your sword, as he moves his right foot in order to place his blade over yours you can strike him with a thrust in quarta (either passing forward with the left foot or with the right).[35] The second is when your sword is in terza; if the opponent advances to gain your sword to the outside, push a thrust in seconda with a pass forward (as above).[36]

STEPS

11 Different masters have different opinions about this subject. Mine is that, to step to the opponent's right side or to his left, you should always move your left foot first, accompanied by the right. To step along the straight line, you may do so by means of gathering steps—both forward or backward. But the best form of footwork is walking naturally, ensuring that the right shoulder leads; the left foot needs to be placed sideways, with the toes pointing left.

---

35 With the right: Capoferro likely alludes at a lunge (as opposed to a left-foot pass).

36 In these examples, Capoferro strays somewhat outside the concept of contratempo as described by his contemporaries (and as he himself describes in paragraph 3 just below): this generally meant giving the opponent an opportunity to strike you (a tempo), so that you could defeat his attack with a well-planned counterattack in single tempo.

STRIKING THE HAND

12 Every time your opponent's sword is out of your presence (high, low, out to your left or to your right), point your sword to his hand in a straight line. Holding your body back, move into measure; once in measure, push a half-tempo thrust to his hand by only bending your body and your right knee forward. After delivering this thrust, retreat with your left foot accompanied by the right. The same course of action and the same strike to the hand can be employed against an opponent who keeps his dagger-arm extended.

RECOVERING AFTER STRIKING

13 After striking the opponent with the extraordinary stance,[37] you need to recover into the ordinary stance. This applies to sword alone, sword and dagger, and sword and cape. This action depends on the amount of room behind you: if this is limited, merely recover your right foot followed by your sword; if you have more room, recover with two backward passes, the last of which will allow you to recover in guard. What I have described is the correct way to recover, although some fencing schools teach other methods.

[37] I.e., a lunging step.

Explanation of Some Practical Fencing Terms

It is important for students to know the terms used by fencing masters as they teach; for this reason, I have decided to include a small compendium that will explain them.

THE SWORD

1 The sword has a forte, a debole, a true and a false edge. Some divide the sword into three equal parts—that is, the debole and the forte at either extremity and a middle part that shares the properties of the other two sections along with their defensive and offensive functions. Others yet divide the sword into four sections, also without any practical reason. All such terms are easy to understand and self-explanatory.

THE GUARDS

2 A guard is commonly understood to be a certain position of the hilt. The hilt forms the prima when it is located higher than the shoulder, the seconda when it is at shoulder-height, the terza when it is lowered to the right and the outside of the knee, and the quarta when it is to the inside of the thigh. These are called the four main guards, and up to this point everyone is pretty much in agreement. But when it comes to the stance, the arm, the torso, the legs, and the direction of the sword, we start hearing different things. Some advocate the narrow stance, others the wide, and others yet the medium. Some keep the arm extended, others hold it more or less withdrawn; some keep the body bent (some forward, some back), some stand in guard with their right foot forward, some[38] with the left. Some keep the sword in a straight line, while others keep it high, low, on either side, forward, or backward—in as many lines as the world has ever seen. And there are those who, depending on the situation, make equal use of all the guards I have just described; according to their properties, these guards are known as high, low, narrow, and wide, or by other whimsical names given to them by the masters.

The terza and quarta are the counter-guards—to gain the opponent's sword to the outside or inside respectively—although all guards can be counter-guards when they are chosen according to the different lines the sword can make.

TEMPO

3 There are four different kinds of tempo commonly used in schools: first tempo, two tempi, half-tempo, and contratempo. First tempo is when I am in measure (narrow or wide) and I can strike the opponent in a single motion of the sword. Two tempi instead require at least two motions of the sword. Half-tempo is either when from wide measure I strike the opponent's extended and uncovered sword-arm or dagger-arm with a cut or a thrust; or when I strike the opponent from the narrow measure as he moves with the intent to strike me or to perform another action. The redoubling of strikes[39] is usually done in half-tempo. The contratempo is when the opponent moves to strike me and I hit him in a shorter measure and tempo. Also, each motion or stillness of the opponent while in measure is considered a tempo.

---

38 Capoferro says "now with the left" (*hora [con] la manca*), making the sentence grammatically shaky.

39 Redoubling of strikes: generally, hitting the opponent additional times in the course of a single fencing action.

MEASURE

4 Measure is either wide or narrow. The first is when I can only strike the opponent through the extraordinary stance; the second is when I can do so from the ordinary stance without moving my feet.

OFFENSIVE TEMPI

5 The following are tempi in which the opponent may be attacked: (1) when he is motionless in guard and then lifts or moves his front foot to approach me; (2) after I parry his attack; (3) when the opponent changes guards with no apparent reason, right after he settles in his new position; (4) when the opponent lifts his hand (as he does so); (5) lastly, when the opponent's strike has passed out of your presence, this is the right tempo to deliver the riposte.

STANCE AND STEPPING

6 Depending on its size, we have the ordinary stance, the extraordinary stance, the regular stance, the half-stance, the narrow, and the wide stance. Stepping can be done by moving forward, back, on either side, obliquely, with one or both legs. There are some who withdraw the front foot when the opponent attacks their leg, and keep it lifted from the ground in order to deliver a quicker riposte.

PARRIES

7 Parries are executed with the true edge and (rarely) with the false edge. They can be executed in the straight line or on oblique lines, with the point high or low, upwards, or downwards—all depending on whether the attack is a cut or a thrust—and can be done with either weapon or with both.[40]

I recommend that all parries be performed with the arm extended and that they be accompanied with the right foot (followed by the left). When you need to employ two tempi, gather your left foot next to the right while you parry and then step forward with your right foot for the riposte.

FEINTS AND COVERING THE SWORD

8 Feints are deceitful motions of the sword that can be performed as cuts or thrusts. They can be executed to the inside, outside, above, or below, forward, backward, and circularly, in the straight line or obliquely, and they can have the purpose of deceiving either of the opponent's weapons. Feints land on the target opposite their initial motion. Counter-feints are performed in response to feints. *Covering the sword* is a sort of feint consisting in covering the opponent's sword-point with your debole, when the opponent is in low quarta. It should be performed in a straight line.

CHANGING GUARDS

9 Changing from one guard to another can be done in three ways: directly, inversely, and alternately. The first case is when I change from prima to seconda, from seconda to terza or from terza to quarta. The second case is the exact opposite. The third is when I change from prima to quarta (or vice-versa), from prima to terza (or vice-versa) or from seconda to quarta (or vice-versa). Be advised that when you change from one guard to another while in measure, it is best to retreat with the left foot accompanied by the right, so as to be safe from the opponent.

40 Meaning the sword and dagger (or even the sword and other companion weapons).

WHAT TO DO AGAINST THOSE WHO CIRCLE[41]

10 It can easily happen that an opponent who circles may gain your sword to the inside; in this case, perform a cavazione at once to the outside, stepping with your left foot (accompanied by your right) obliquely towards the opponent's right, and place your sword in a straight line against the opponent's right shoulder. If he tries to gain your sword again to the outside, as he moves to do so, perform a cavazione under his sword and strike him with a thrust in quarta with an accrescimento of the right foot.

WHAT TO DO AGAINST A LEFT-FOOT-FORWARD GUARD

11 If your opponent is situated in low terza with his left foot forward, set yourself also in terza, but with your right foot forward and the point of your sword making an angle to your left. I recommend this position for two reasons: first, by doing this you prevent him from gaining your sword with his dagger; second, the greater opening you show creates an invitation for him to attack you with a pass. If he does perform the passing attack, parry in terza with the sword (point high), pass and strike him with a dagger-thrust to the chest.

If instead you wish to attack an opponent situated in the left-foot-forward guard, you should set yourself in terza with your sword in straight line, ensuring that your blade points at the opponent's dagger-hand. This enables you to do several things. Firstly, you can strike him with a half-tempo thrust to the hand. Also, you can perform a feint above his dagger; if he tries to parry, perform a cavazione under his hand, pass forward with your left foot and, placing your dagger against his sword, strike him under his arm. Lastly, you can perform a feint under his dagger; if he tries to parry, perform a cavazione and strike him in seconda above the dagger, passing and parrying as above. Actually, the feint and strike could also be performed without the pass. In this case, after the feint you would need to wait for the opponent to pass and perform his attack; as he does so, slightly withdraw your body, parry with the dagger and strike him above or below his sword (as the occasion calls for).

If you are fencing a left-hander who stands in a right-foot-forward guard, you should face him with your left foot forward, your sword low and withdrawn and your body bent towards your right. Also bring your weapons to your right side, which will make the opponent unable to perform any attack without encountering your defenses.

GAINING THE SWORD

12 Gaining the opponent's sword is done either to advance into measure, or to uncover the opponent to the inside, outside, above, or below—but always in a straight line—while he moves or is stationary. This technique is most often performed in two tempi: in the first tempo, gain the opponent's debole with a palmo of yours; in the second, as the opponent performs a cavazione, begin gaining his forte with or without a controcavazione.

Make sure you perform these actions in a straight line, and that the forte always accompanies the debole and the motion of your foot.

[41] *Girare*. In this context, likely, the act of moving off-line to find a better angle from which to gain the opponent's sword. This is not to be taken as "circling around the opponent," something completely absent in this art.

IMPORTANT ADVICE ABOUT CONTROLLING THE OPPONENT'S SWORD[42]

13 There are two ways in which you can control the opponent's sword. The first is that, after you gain his sword, you strike him without ever relinquishing control of his blade. The second is that you beat the opponent's sword in any manner so as to momentarily push it out of presence: while his sword moves propelled by your beat it is considered to be in your control, because you should use that tempo to strike the opponent before he can recover.

In sword alone, the control of the opponent's sword can be related to motion or stillness, to the thrust or the cut. You may control the opponent's sword with your forte while parrying, or you may beat it with your debole to find a tempo or the measure. After gaining control of the opponent's sword with your forte, you should never riposte with a cut, but always with the thrust.

In sword and dagger, on the other hand, you may gain control of his sword with both weapons together—since the dagger serves as further insurance for this control. But even in this case, my recommendation is to always strike with the thrust, since it is more lethal and it does not entail removing your sword from presence, which is just the opposite of the cut.

THE CAVAZIONE AND CONTROCAVAZIONE

14 The cavazione and the controcavazione are actions performed to gain measure and the tempo, or to prevent the opponent from doing the same. Depending on the reason, they should be performed (respectively) with a forward motion or a backward motion. The same reasons dictate how the controcavazione is performed, following the motion of the opponent's sword until yours is where it started. All this can be done either on the inside or the outside.

When you perform a cavazione with the purpose of gaining the opponent's sword, you may do so by going either below or above his blade. When you go below, do so with your arm extended and with a little advance of your right foot. When you go above, slightly withdraw your body and keep your arm and sword at a backward-sloping angle: as soon as your sword has cleared the opponent's point, immediately place your forte over his blade. This type of cavazione can be done to strike or to gain the opponent's sword.

STRIKES

15 Strikes fall into two categories: cuts and thrusts. In turn, cuts and thrusts can be of different kinds, depending on the nature of the strike. The mandritto and the riverso can be regular, *fendente, tondo, montante, stramazzone,* or *ridoppio*. Thrusts are instead divided into four classes.

The *mandritto*[43] starts from your right side. The regular mandritto follows a slanted path from the opponent's left shoulder to his right knee. The *fendente* proceeds vertically downwards, while the *tondo* strikes horizontally. The *montante* is delivered upward with the true edge and it ends at the opponent's right shoulder. The *stramazzone* is a wheel-like cut delivered from the wrist. The ridoppio (as it is usually known) is a half-mandritto that beats down the opponent's sword followed by a regular mandritto.

The *falso* may be of two kinds—dritto or manco. The *falso dritto* can be used to beat the opponent's sword out of line towards his right, while the *falso manco* performs this function in the opposite direction. In my opinion, attacks that would normally call for a falso dritto as a parry would be best thwarted by turning the wrist and performing the parry with the true edge: this parry is safer and more conducive to a quick true-edge riposte. Conversely, when you parry an attack with a falso manco you may riposte both with a cut and a thrust.

---

42 Controlling the opponent's sword: *dominare la spada.*

43 Note that although Capoferro has just stated that there are four classes of thrust, he now returns to defining the cuts. The four thrusts are described in paragraph 17.

Remember that false-edge parries are performed with the debole, while true-edge parries are performed with the forte. Also, please be advised that mandritti and riversi are delivered from the elbow and (tempo and measure allowing) with the help of the upper arm.

THE CUT

16 Cuts should be executed with a saw-like motion, thereby allowing the whole debole to perform the strike. Also, by doing so, the sharpest part of the blade is gradually brought to bear. For this reason, cuts that go all the way down are more powerful than those that stop somewhere from the waist up: the upper and lower body are differently suited to be stricken in measure with saw-like cuts.

THE THRUST

17 The *stoccata*, the *imbroccata* and the *punta riversa* are the thrusts commonly mentioned.

The *imbroccata* starts from the guard of prima and strikes the opponent anywhere between his left shoulder and right knee. The imbroccata is performed with the false edge facing down: do not turn your hand until the point is on target. This thrust is normally executed with a vigorous arm-extension.

The *stoccata* starts from the guard of terza and strikes in the direction of the opponent's right shoulder. The *punta riversa,* instead, starts from the guard of quarta and strikes to the outside of the opponent's shoulder, with the hand well turned to the inside.

Lastly, some describe the *punta in falso,* which is an ascending thrust aimed at the opponent's chest delivered from a low guard.

Plate 1

How to Unsheathe the Sword

Since different countries have different customs, hostilities can often be accompanied by insincerity. Therefore, teaching you how to unsheathe the sword may not be out of place before we move on to its use, so that you may be ready for any situation.

If you happen to have your right foot forward as you get ready to unsheathe the sword (as one of the two fencers in the illustration), you must pull your right foot back, at the same time extending your arm in a high prima. If instead you happen to have your left foot forward (like the other fencer in the illustration), merely unsheathe the sword as described without moving your feet.

The best way to unsheathe the sword in sword and cape, sword and dagger or even sword alone is to present the sword in quarta with the right foot forward or, if the opponent is near, to draw the left foot back while presenting the sword as described. In this manner, the point of your sword keeps the opponent at a distance while you set your weapons in guard. This will suffice on the matter of unsheathing the sword.

Plate 2

Plate 3

Plate 4

Explanation of the Guards

Just as good and judicious writing cannot happen without the letters of the alphabet, the art of fencing cannot be explained without the following guards and a number of voids. These are the fundamentals of our discipline, and without them, we could not illustrate the practice of fencing.

So, in these six figures marked by letters, A represents the guard of prima, B the seconda, C the terza, D the quarta, E the quinta, and F the sesta.

Plate 5

Figure Explained by Letters

Showing both the guard (according to the principles of our art) and the incredible extension of the lunge, in relation to the parts of the body which all coordinate to perform the strike.

A. The left shoulder while in guard

B. The left knee while in guard

C. The sole of the left foot while in guard

D. The regular stance while in guard

E. The sole of the right foot while in guard

F. The thigh and the sloping leg while in guard

G. The right hand while in guard

H. The extension of the right arm (equal to its length)

I. The extension of the right knee (almost equal to your stance[44])

K. The extension of the stance (a little over a shoe-length)

L. The extension of the left foot and the turn it makes

M. The extension of the left knee (equal to half of your stance[45])

---

44 Meaning your stance while in guard.

45 See previous note.

Plate 6

How to Gain the Opponent's Sword In a Straight Line to the Inside

And how to strike according to the placement of the opponent's sword.[46]

I see two reasons to press the opponent: the first is to gain his sword in order to seek the measure and tempo. The second is to advance against him just to gain the measure. Both these actions can be performed in a straight line.

These two reasons, in turn, pertain to two different situations. Gaining the opponent's sword to seek the measure and tempo should be done when the opponent is in quarta with his sword angled towards your left; if you are to the outside, perform a cavazione with an accrescimento, so as to gain his sword in a straight line to the inside (as shown in the illustration). This should not be difficult, since if the opponent's blade is at an angle, it is enough that you proceed in a straight line to successfully gain his sword. Advancing to gain the measure, instead, should be done when the opponent's sword is in a straight line or when it leaves his body open; in this case, it is enough to advance with the sword against his body, also in a straight line. Even without gaining his sword, this action is sufficient to seek the tempo and then strike him depending on the placement of his sword, although in common practice they teach to gain the opponent's sword in different lines (for no reason whatsoever).

Here is the explanation of the concept of striking according to the placement of the opponent's sword. When the opponent's sword-point is in your presence, you can strike him in a straight line, and it is the height of his point that dictates the placement of your thrust. This type of thrust is very safe, so long as you take care to take a palmo of his debole with your forte. For instance, if his point is as high as your head, you will strike him in the face; if it is as high as your torso, you can strike him either in the face or in the chest. This is why this technique is called "striking according to the placement of the opponent's sword." Furthermore, this technique makes it safe to perform cavazioni to either side in order to strike the opponent—again, as long as you take the opponent's point with your forte in the first tempo of the action.

[46] Strike according to the placement of the opponent's sword: *ferire secondo il punto.*

Do not act like some masters, who perform or teach cavazioni to strike in the first tempo and, without realizing it, place their own point right into the opponent's forte; by doing so, they give the opponent a good opportunity to strike them through their debole, which is often the result of the action (as you will see in the following illustrations).

Plate 7

This Illustration and the Following Show Various Ways to Strike to the Outside, After You Have Gained the Opponent's Blade to the Inside and He Performs a Thrusting Attack by Cavazione

As the explanation of the following illustration, you (D) gain the blade of your opponent (C) to the inside. He performs a cavazione to attack you with a thrust to the chest, and you strike him with a thrust to the left eye, either with no step or with an accrescimento (as shown).

A prudent opponent would act as follows. He would feint the cavazione while keeping his body somewhat back. When you come forward for your attack, he would perform an outside parry (with the false or true edge), and give you a mandritto to your face or an imbroccata to the chest. He would then recover in a low quarta.

Practical Synopsis of Plate 7

- Starting position: agent and patient in terza to the inside

Sequence A

1. Agent: gains the patient's sword, turning his hand in quarta
2. Patient: performs a cavazione to the outside and pushes a thrust to the agent's chest (with the hand in seconda or seconda-terza)
3. Agent: parries the patient's attack by turning his hand in seconda and counterthrusting (either with or without a lunge)

Sequence B

1. Agent: gains the patient's sword, turning his hand in quarta
2. Patient: performs a feint by cavazione to the outside, keeping his body withdrawn
3. Agent: believing the feint, attacks with a counterthrust in seconda
4. Patient: parries the agent's attack with the true or false edge and ripostes with either a mandritto to the agent's face or an imbroccata to his chest; patient recovers in low quarta

Plate 8

Illustration Showing how Much Measure Is Lost in an Attack to the Legs

You (D) gain the blade of your opponent (C), and he turns a riverso to your leg. You can strike him with a stramazzone to the arm while he turns his cut, or with a thrust to the face made easier by his excessive forward motion (as shown). Make sure you pull your right leg back as you strike.

A prudent opponent would act as follows: As you gain his blade, he would let loose a riverso to your face, accompanied by a mandritto fendente to your head. This would be a safer action.

Practical Synopsis of Plate 8

- Starting position: agent and patient in terza to the inside

Sequence A

1. Agent: gains the patient's sword, turning his hand in quarta
2. Patient: attacks the agent with a riverso to the leg
3. Agent: performs a void by passing back with his right foot and strikes the patient in contratempo with either a stramazzone to the arm or a thrust to the face

Sequence B

1. Agent: gains the patient's sword, turning his hand in quarta
2. Patient: performs a cavazione to the outside, simultaneously executing a riverso to the agent's head
3. [Agent: lifts his hand in seconda or terza to parry the riverso]
4. Patient: reverses the direction of the cut into a mandritto fendente to the agent's head

Plate 9

Strike with a Pass while the Opponent Attacks with a Cavazione

You (D) gain the sword of your opponent (C) to the inside. He performs a cavazione to attack you with a thrust to the face, and you strike him in the face in seconda with a pass, while executing a left-hand grapple to his hilt.

A prudent opponent would act as follows. He would feint the cavazione while keeping his body somewhat back. As you attack with a pass, he would perform a cavazione under your blade, execute an inquartata with his left foot crossed behind his right, and strike you in the chest.

Practical Synopsis of Plate 9

- Starting position: agent and patient in terza to the inside

Sequence A

1. Agent: gains the patient's sword, turning his hand in quarta
2. Patient: performs a cavazione to the outside and attempts a strike in seconda
3. Agent: parries the patient's attack while turning his hand in seconda and delivers a thrust in contratempo by passing forward with his left foot and grasping the opponent's hilt

Sequence B

1. Agent: gains the patient's sword, turning his hand in quarta
2. Patient: performs a feint by cavazione, keeping his body withdrawn
3. Agent: believing the feint, attempts a thrust in contratempo by passing forward with his left foot
4. Patient: frees his sword by means of a cavazione to the inside (with the hand in quarta), voids the agent's attack by means of an inquartata and strikes the agent to the chest

Plate 10

Strike in Quarta in the Pit of the Right Arm while the Opponent Attacks with a Cavazione

You (D) gain the sword of your opponent (C), he turns a riverso to your face, and you strike him in quarta during the turn of his cut. Make sure that you lift your arm and your hilt, and that you perform a good accrescimento as you strike his chest under his sword-arm, as shown.

Instead of the riverso, the opponent could perform a cavazione and hold back, with somewhat of a retreat, while lifting his sword in an oblique line pointing to your left. As you attack in quarta, he would parry with a half-mandritto and follow with a riverso to your face or a thrust to your chest.

Practical Synopsis of Plate 10

- Starting position: agent and patient in terza to the inside

Sequence A

1. Agent: gains the patient's sword, turning his hand in quarta
2. Patient: performs a cavazione to the outside and attacks with a riverso to the face
3. Agent: with his hand in quarta, delivers a strike in contratempo under the patient's sword-arm, keeping his hilt high and performing an accrescimento

Sequence B

1. Agent: gains the patient's sword, turning his hand in quarta
2. Patient: performs a cavazione to the outside, keeping his point high and directed at the agent's left side—while maintaining his body withdrawn
3. Agent: with his hand in quarta, delivers a strike under the patient's sword-arm
4. Patient: parries the agent's attack with a half-mandritto and delivers a riposte in the form of a riverso to the face or thrust to the chest

Plate 11

Various Actions Ending with a Strike Below the Opponent's Sword

First action. From the terza guard, set yourself in a high, angled quarta, so that your point is directed at the opponent's left shoulder. As he comes to cover your sword with an oblique line, turn your hand in seconda, bend your body low and strike him in contratempo to the torso, below his blade, as pictured.

Second action. If the opponent gains your sword to the outside, perform a feint by cavazione in quarta to his face; as he attempts a parry, turn your hand, bend your body and strike him below his blade, as described.

Third action. If he gains your sword to the inside, perform a feint by cavazione in terza to his face; as he lifts his sword while attempting a parry, strike him below his blade, turning your hand in seconda in the manner described.

Fourth action. If you gain his blade to the inside, and he performs a cavazione to attack you with a thrust to the face, you can strike him in two ways. The first is in contratempo as he comes forward, taking care to lower your body and to have your sword in terza. The second is by parrying in terza with your point high, then turning your hand into seconda as you strike him in the same way described above.

Fifth and last action. If you gain the opponent's sword to the outside, he may perform a cavazione to gain yours to the inside. In that tempo, turn your hand, lower your body and strike him in terza below his sword, as described.

Practical Synopsis of Plate 11

Sequence A

- Starting position: agent and patient in terza to the inside

1. Agent: turns his hand into a high quarta, angling his sword towards the opponent's left shoulder
2. Patient: attempts to gain the agent's sword
3. Agent: delivers a thrust of low seconda to the opponent's right flank, bending his body for added safety

Sequence B

- Starting position: agent and patient in terza to the outside

1. Agent: gains the patient's sword to the outside, his hand in seconda
2. Patient: performs a cavazione to the inside, together with a feint in quarta to the agent's face
3. Agent: believes the feint and attempts an inside parry
4. Patient: lowers his sword and body under the opponent's blade and delivers the attack in seconda to the agent's flank

Sequence C

- Starting position: agent and patient in terza to the inside

1. Agent: gains the patient's sword, turning his hand in quarta
2. Patient: performs a feint by cavazione to the outside
3. Agent: believing the feint, attempts a parry [with the hand in seconda or terza]
4. Patient: lowers his sword and body under the opponent's blade and delivers the attack in seconda to the agent's flank

Sequence D

- Starting position: agent and patient in terza to the inside

1. Agent: gains the opponent's sword, turning his hand in quarta
2. Patient: performs a cavazione to the outside and attacks in seconda

3a. Agent (contratempo action): strikes in contratempo by lowering his body and his sword in terza, hitting the patient in the flank

3b. Agent (parry and riposte): parries the patient's attack with his hand in terza, and ripostes to the opponent's flank with a thrust in low seconda

Sequence E

- Starting position: agent and patient in terza to the outside

1. Agent: gains the opponent's sword, turning his hand in seconda
2. Patient: performs a cavazione to find the agent's sword to the inside [turning his hand in quarta]
3. Agent: takes the tempo of the opponent's cavazione and delivers a thrust in low seconda to the patient's flank

Plate 12

Sword-Parry with Both Hands, Strike to the Throat with a Left-Foot Pass During the Opponent's Cavazione

You (D) gain the sword of your opponent (C) to the inside, in a low guard, and he performs a cavazione to attack you with a thrust to the chest. You pass forward with your left foot, and in the same tempo use both hands to press down on the opponent's sword, striking him in the chest in terza.

Undoubtedly, a knowledgeable opponent would act as follows. As he performs the cavazione with his point to strike you, he would somewhat hold the point back. When you parry and pass forward with both hands on your sword to attack him, he would only need to lower his point towards the ground, turn his hand in seconda, void with his body to your left side, perform a cavazione *di filo*[47] above your blade and strike your face to the inside with a riverso. He would then recover in terza.

Or, after parrying, he would pass with his left foot towards the inside, to the right,[48] executing a turn with the body. As he turns, he would grasp his sword with both hands and strike you with a thrust to the chest while he goes against you, and you would not be able to defend yourself.

---

[47] *Filo* is Italian for "edge." This action is likely a cavazione over the opponent's blade that starts with the blade-contact between the opponent's sword in seconda (point down) and yours in terza, whereby contact between your edge (or *filo*) and the opponent's sword is maintained until the cut is performed.

[48] *Alla destra*: Capoferro likely means towards your (his adversary's) right side.

Practical Synopsis of Plate 12

- Starting position: agent and patient in terza to the inside

Sequence A

1. Agent: gains the patient's sword, turning his hand in low quarta
2. Patient: performs a cavazione and attacks the agent with a thrust to the chest
3. Agent: defends by placing his forte over the opponent's debole, using both hands to press his sword down against the opponent's; delivers a thrust in terza to the opponent's chest while passing forward with the left foot

Sequence B

1. Agent: gains the patient's sword, turning his hand into low quarta
2. Patient: performs a feint by cavazione to the agent's chest, keeping his body withdrawn
3. Agent: believing the feint, performs the action described in point 3 above

4a. Patient: lowers his point, voids his body towards his right, performs a cavazione above the opponent's blade and releases a riverso to the agent's face; recovers in terza

4b. Patient: parries the agent's attack, then passes with his left foot and, grasping his sword with both hands, delivers a thrust to the agent's chest

Plate 13

Strike of *Scannatura* – A Thrust to the Right Flank with a Left-Foot Pass while the Opponent Attacks with a Cavazione

This strike is called a *scannatura*,[49] and here is how it is performed. You (C) gain the sword of your opponent (D) to the outside. He performs a cavazione and attacks you with a thrust to the face. You set his sword aside to the outside,[50] lower your point in seconda, pass forward with your left foot and strike him in the flank in the same tempo. You also use your body to lower his hilt, and grab his hand as depicted.

49 In this case, a thrust going through the target sideways.

50 This is the first of three of actions in which Capoferro uses the equivalent of a circular parry to the outside, i.e., a parry in which the action starts to the inside, then the defender circles his blade to the outside (essentially a tight cavazione) and executes a simple parry, followed by a riposte to the flank. This parry is called by Capoferro *affrontare la spada*. See glossary for more information.

Practical Synopsis of Plate 13

- Starting position: to the outside—agent in terza, patient in quarta

Sequence A

1. Agent: gains the patient's sword with his hand in terza
2. Patient: performs a cavazione to the inside, attempting a thrust to the agent's face
3. Agent: parries the patient's attack with a circular parry to the outside and strikes the patient in the flank with a pass of low seconda. While doing so, grasps the patient's hilt for added safety and presses it down by lowering his body.

Plate 14

Strike in Contratempo Under the Opponent's Sword with a Low-Line Void and No Parry

You (D) gain the sword of your opponent (C) to the inside. He performs a cavazione to attack you with a thrust to the face. You lower your body, perform an accrescimento with your right leg in the same tempo, and strike him in contratempo under his sword in seconda (as depicted).

There is another way to end this action with a thrust.

The opponent performs a cavazione to attack you with a thrust to the face. You parry in terza with your point high, then, in the same tempo, you lower your point, turn your sword in seconda and strike him in the chest with a left-foot pass while grasping his sword-hand.

An experienced opponent would do the following. He would pull his right foot back and, as you come forward, he would set aside your sword to the outside. In the same tempo, he would lower his point, turn his hand in seconda and strike you with a *scannatura* under your sword. Also, he could pull his right foot back, parry downwards with his left hand under his arm and strike you with a high seconda to the chest or face.

Practical Synopsis of Plate 14

- Starting position: agent and patient in terza to the inside

Sequence A

1. Agent: gains the patient's sword, turning his hand in quarta
2. Patient: performs a cavazione and an attack to the outside [hand in seconda]
3. Agent: without parrying, lowers his body and strikes the patient in seconda to the flank

Sequence B (with parry and riposte in two tempi)

1. Agent: gains the patient's sword, turning his hand in quarta
2. Patient: performs a cavazione and an attack to the outside [hand in seconda]
3. Agent: parries the patient's attack with a circular parry in terza with the point high, then ripostes in seconda to the opponent's chest, passing with the left foot and grasping the patient's sword-hand

Sequence C

1. Agent: gains the patient's sword, turning his hand in quarta
2. Patient: performs a cavazione and an attack to the outside [hand in seconda]
3. Agent: parries the patient's attack in terza with the point high, and attempts the riposte of seconda described above in point 3

4a. Patient: voids by passing back with his right foot and uses his left hand to parry the agent's thrust downward while delivering a thrust in seconda under the agent's sword

4b. Patient: voids by passing back with his right foot and uses his left hand to parry the agent's thrust to the right, while delivering a thrust in high seconda to the agent's face or chest

Plate 15

Two Ways to Gain Your Opponent's Sword, to the Inside and Outside

I know by experience how incredibly useful it is to know how to gain the opponent's sword. This is why I thought it would be important to describe how to do it. When gaining the opponent's sword to the inside or outside (as the situation requires), begin by gaining a palmo of his blade, noting that your sword points to your opponent's right shoulder when gaining to the inside and at his left shoulder when gaining to the outside. Having accomplished this, advance toward your opponent's sword; if he performs a cavazione as you advance, perform a controcavazione, either to return to your starting position, or to strike in the tempo of his cavazione.

If your opponent comes to gain your sword (to the inside or the outside), while your blade is parallel to the ground and held in a straight line with the arm extended, in that instant, perform a cavazione and gain his sword while advancing:

- If you perform a cavazione to gain his sword to the inside, as you make the cavazione, step forward with your right foot, bend your body to the right, and bring your left hand near your right; then pass with your left foot and strike him in the chest with a thrust in quarta.

- If you perform a cavazione to gain his sword to the outside, simultaneously step forward with your right foot and bend your body to the left; then pass with your left foot and strike him in the chest in seconda.

Note that the following illustration shows the sword being gained in terza to the outside. So, use the method described above to gain the opponent's blade.

Plate 16

This Illustration and the Following Ones Show Various Ways to Strike the Opponent to the Inside Always Assuming the Action Starts to the Outside with You Finding His Blade and He Attacking with a Cavazione

The following illustrations show various ways to strike to the inside. These assume, on your part, that you gain his blade to the outside, and on his part, that he attacks with a cavazione.

In this case, your opponent (D) performs a cavazione as described, and you strike him in the throat or face without any footwork or with an accrescimento.

If the opponent had been more knowledgeable, he would have beaten your sword with his edge after his cavazione and attacked you with a thrust to the face or a riverso to the arm. He would have then recovered in terza in the ordinary stance.

Practical Synopsis of Plate 16

- Starting position: to the outside—agent in terza, patient in quarta

Sequence A

1. Agent: gains the opponent's sword with his hand in terza
2. Patient: performs a cavazione and attempts a thrust in quarta
3. Agent: strikes the patient in contratempo with a thrust in quarta to the throat

Sequence B

1. Agent: gains the opponent's sword with his hand in terza
2. Patient: performs a cavazione to the inside and beats the agent's sword, attacks the agent with a thrust to the face or a riverso to the arm and recovers in terza

Plate 17

Strike Near the Ear, with a Right-Foot Void

You (C) have gained the sword of your opponent (B) to the outside. The opponent performs a cavazione to attack you in quarta; you strike him near the ear, with an oblique step of the right foot outside of the path of his sword.

An experienced opponent would act in the following manner. He would feint the cavazione while holding his body somewhat back, and as you come forward with your attack and an oblique void of the right foot, he would set your blade aside from the outside and lower his point in seconda. In the same tempo, he would pass forward with his left foot, strike you in the flank and grab your sword-hand.

Practical Synopsis of Plate 17

- Starting position: to the outside—agent in terza, patient in seconda

Sequence A

1. Agent: gains the patient's sword in terza
2. Patient: performs a cavazione to the inside and attacks with a thrust in quarta
3. Agent: voids the opponent's thrust by stepping at an angle with his right foot and delivers a thrust in contratempo with his hand in quarta

Sequence B

1. Agent: gains the patient's sword in terza
2. Patient: performs a feint by cavazione to the inside, keeping his body back
3. Agent: believing the feint, attempts the strike in contratempo (see point 3 above)
4. Patient: performs a circular parry to the outside and delivers a thrust in low seconda with a left-foot pass, while grabbing the opponent's sword-hand

Plate 18

Strike in Quarta to the Throat, with a Pass of the Left Foot

You (C) gain the sword of your opponent (B) to the outside. He performs a cavazione to attack you with a thrust to the face, but while he performs the cavazione you strike his throat or face in quarta with a pass of the left foot (as pictured).

Here is what a more experienced opponent would do. He would feint a cavazione while keeping his body back, and as you pass forward to strike him in quarta, he would perform a void (inquartata), pass with his left foot behind his right and strike you in the chest.

Practical Synopsis of Plate 18

- Starting position: to the outside—agent in terza, patient in seconda

Sequence A

1. Agent: gains the patient's sword in terza
2. Patient: performs a cavazione to the inside and attacks the agent with a thrust to the face
3. Agent: delivers a thrust in contratempo to the patient's throat or face, with his hand in quarta while passing with his left foot

Sequence B

1. Agent: gains the patient's sword in terza
2. Patient: performs a feint by cavazione to the inside, keeping his body back
3. Agent: believing the feint, attempts the thrust in contratempo (see point 3 above)
4. Patient: voids the agent's thrust with an inquartata, striking him in quarta to the chest

Plate 19

Strike in Quarta and Void, with the Left Foot Crossed Behind the Right

You (C) gain the blade of your opponent (D) to the outside. He performs a cavazione and attacks you with a thrust to the face. You strike him in quarta with a body-void, passing with your left foot crossed behind your right, as shown in the illustration.

A judicious opponent would do the following. He would perform a cavazione to gain your blade to the inside, while bending his body to his right. After doing this, he would immediately pass forward with his left foot and attack you with a thrust in quarta to your chest. He could also perform a cavazione, beat your sword with a half-mandritto, give you a riverso to the face and retreat in terza. This would keep him safe.

Practical Synopsis of Plate 19

- Starting position: to the outside—agent in terza, patient in quarta

Sequence A

1. Agent: gains the opponent's sword in terza
2. Patient: performs a cavazione to the inside and attacks the agent with a thrust to the face
3. Agent: eludes the patient's attack with an inquartata, thus voiding with the body, while delivering a thrust in contratempo in quarta

Sequence B

1. Agent: gains the opponent's sword in terza
2. Patient: performs a cavazione and gains the agent's sword in quarta to the inside, bending his body towards his right; strikes the agent in the chest with a pass in quarta

Sequence C

1. Agent: gains the opponent's sword in terza
2. Patient: performs a cavazione to the inside, beats the agent's sword with a half-mandritto, turns a riverso to the agent's face and recovers in terza

Plate 20

Strike to the Opponent's Face with a Pass in Seconda and a Left-Hand Grab of His Sword-Arm

Here is the explanation of the action in this illustration. You (C) gain the opponent's sword (D) to the outside. He performs a cavazione to strike you with a thrust. You parry in quarta while executing a beat with your right foot; then, in one tempo, you pass forward and, turning your body, you strike him with a seconda to the face. You could do the same without passing, striking him in quarta also in two tempi.

Here is what an opponent with more fencing experience would do. As you (C) perform a cavazione to parry his (D's) thrust while executing a beat with your right foot, he would perform a controcavazione to the outside.[51] He would then strike you with a seconda to the face and recover back in terza, ensuring that his sword follows yours. In this scenario, it is C (you) that would receive the hit.

[51] This alternative sequence contains an inconsistency with the previous one, since it is figure D (the opponent), and not you, who performs the first cavazione to the inside, making it unnecessary for you to also perform a cavazione in order to parry in quarta. Sequence B of the practical synopsis is adjusted to reflect your (C's) cavazione. Alternatively, you could start sequence B from the outside, and do away with the cavazione in step 3.

Practical Synopsis of Plate 20

Sequence A

- Starting position: to the outside—agent in terza, patient in quarta

1. Agent: gains the patient's sword in terza
2. Patient: performs a cavazione to the inside and attempts to strike the agent with a thrust in quarta

3a. Agent: parries the agent's thrust in quarta while performing a beat with his right foot and, passing with his left foot and turning his body, strikes the patient in the face with a seconda while grasping his sword-arm with the left hand

3b. Agent: parries the agent's thrust in quarta while performing a beat with his right foot and delivers a riposte in quarta with a lunge

Sequence B

- Starting position: to the inside (see footnote)—agent in terza, patient in quarta

1. Agent: gains the patient's sword
2. Patient: performs a feint by cavazione to the outside
3. Agent: performs a cavazione to the inside and parries in quarta while beating his right foot
4. Patient: performs the controcavazione to the outside and strikes the agent in the face with a seconda. Recovers in terza.

Plate 21

How to Gain the Opponent's Sword in a High Prima to the Inside, with the Sword and Dagger; If His Sword Points to Your Right Shoulder, You Should Do So to the Outside; the Same Applies for Gaining Low Guards

These fencers show you the play of sword and dagger and, specifically, how to gain the opponent's sword if you are in high prima. It is impossible to use a single illustration to display all the ways to gain the opponent's sword to the inside and outside, from above and below; I will leave this to the reader's judgment.

If the opponent's point is aimed to your right side, gain his blade to the outside. To gain the opponent's sword when it is in a low guard, you must keep your blade at a downward[52] angle, both against the terza and the quarta.

[52] Downward: *pendiculare* is, in this context, a slightly problematic word. It could mean downward, but also "perpendicular," which in this case may also apply to the angle it forms with the opponent's blade. I strongly favor the first interpretation.

Plate 22

How a Single Dagger-Parry Enables You to Deliver a Thrust in Three Different Places: the Face, the Chest, and the Thigh

This illustration shows an artistic way to perform a single dagger-parry that enables you to strike the opponent with a thrust to three different targets.

Gain the opponent's sword to the inside in quarta, in whatever position is suitable to gain the opponent's blade to the inside. As he performs a cavazione to attack you to the face or chest, parry with the dagger to the inside[53] over your right arm.

Against his attack to your face, you can strike him high or low, i.e., to the face, to the chest (under his arm), or to the leg. Against his attack to your chest, you can only strike him to the face or thigh.

Practical Synopsis of Plate 22

- Starting position: agent and patient to the inside

Sequence A

1. Agent: gains the patient's sword with his sword-hand in quarta
2. Patient: performs a cavazione to free his sword and strike the agent to the face
3. Agent: uses his dagger over his right arm to parry the patient's thrust and delivers a thrust to one of three targets
    - to the patient's face
    - to the patient's chest
    - to the patient's thigh

53 When describing dagger parries, "inside" means a left-to right motion of the dagger, "outside" the opposite.

Sequence B

1. Agent: finds the patient's sword with his sword-hand in quarta
2. Patient: performs a cavazione to free his sword and strike the agent to the chest
3. Agent: uses his dagger over his right arm to parry the patient's thrust and delivers a thrust to one of two targets
   - to the patient's face
   - to the patient's thigh

Plate 23

Feint, Cavazione Above the Dagger and Strike in Seconda to the Chest Between the Weapons; or Strike in Quarta

If the opponent is in a low terza with his sword-arm withdrawn and the dagger extended and joined to his sword, proceed in this manner.

Face him in a high terza. Perform a feint towards his face in high quarta or terza to the outside of his dagger. As he lifts his dagger to parry while attempting a strike in quarta, perform a cavazione above his dagger, parry to the inside and strike him to the chest in seconda.

Practical Synopsis of Plate 23

- Starting position: agent in high terza, patient in low terza with his arm withdrawn, his dagger extended, and the sword joined to it

1. Agent: executes a feint in high quarta or terza to the outside of the patient's dagger
2. Patient: believing the feint, attempts a dagger-parry and a strike in contratempo in quarta
3. Agent: parries to the inside while striking the patient to the chest in seconda

Plate 24

Strike to the Chest Above the Right Arm and Disarm by Forcing His Weapon with Your Sword and Dagger

This illustration will easily show you and teach you how to disarm the opponent while striking him with a thrust to the chest at the same time.

If you are in terza with your arm withdrawn and your dagger joined to your sword, and your opponent is in the same guard or in quarta, proceed in this manner.

Find his sword in quarta to the inside while letting your dagger get level with the middle of your right arm, holding it at an oblique angle. When he performs a cavazione to attack you in quarta to the chest, strike him to the outside[54] with a punta riversa in quarta to the body. Lift your hilt and, at the same time, parry downwards with the flat of your dagger (to the outside of the dagger). This will force him to relinquish his weapon.

Practical Synopsis of Plate 24

- Starting position: to the inside. Agent in terza with his sword-arm withdrawn and the dagger joined to the sword; patient in the same guard or in quarta

1. Agent: gains the patient's sword to the inside in quarta, while lowering his dagger to the middle of his own right arm, to invite an attack above the dagger
2. Patient: performs a cavazione to the outside and makes an attack in quarta to the agent's chest
3. Agent: strikes the patient in quarta over his arm but under his hilt, while simultaneously parrying downward and to the left with the dagger. The combined effect of the sword pushing up and the dagger pushing down will force the patient to drop his weapon.

---

54 The illustration does not quite match the text: it should show your blade going under (rather than over) the opponent's sword and then over his forearm. This is what affords you the necessary leverage to perform the disarm. Also, this would be the position of your sword after he performs his cavazione to the outside, while for you to end up above his blade would require that your sword be on the inside.

Plate 25

High Dagger-Parry to the Inside, Riverso to the Thigh and Quarta to the Chest as Illustrated

If you are in quarta with your dagger high, and your opponent is in any guard suitable for gaining your sword to the inside (right foot forward), proceed in this manner.

Gain his sword to the inside in quarta. As he performs a cavazione to strike you to the face in quarta, parry to the inside with your dagger above your right arm. Strike him with a riverso to the thigh or with a quarta under his arm.

Practical Synopsis of Plate 25

- Starting position: to the inside—agent in quarta with the dagger high, patient in any right-foot-forward guard suitable for gaining the opponent's blade to the inside

1. Agent: starts to gain the patient's sword to the inside in quarta
2. Patient: performs a cavazione and attacks to the face in quarta

3a. Agent: executes a dagger-parry over his right arm, attacks with a riverso to the thigh

3b. Agent: as above, attacks with thrust in quarta below the patient's arm

Plate 26

Parry with the Sword in Quarta, Accompanied by the Dagger; Strike to the Face in Quarta or Riverso to the Arm, as Illustrated

If you happen to be in an extended terza with your dagger close to your right wrist, and your opponent is in any guard suitable for gaining your sword to the outside, proceed in this manner.

Begin by gaining his sword in terza—high or low depending on the situation—without moving your dagger from its current location. As the opponent performs a cavazione to attack you in quarta or seconda, parry with your sword in quarta, accompanied by your dagger. As you see, you can strike him with a riverso to the arm or with a quarta to the face.

PRACTICAL SYNOPSIS OF PLATE 26

- Starting position: to the outside—agent in extended terza with his dagger to his right wrist, patient in any guard suitable for gaining the blade to the outside

1. Agent: starts to gain the patient's sword to the outside in terza (high or low as needed), without moving the dagger
2. Patient: performs a cavazione and attacks the agent to the face in quarta or seconda

3a. Agent: parries with the sword and quarta together with the dagger, ripostes with a riverso to the arm

3b. Agent: parries with the sword in quarta together with the dagger, counterthrusts in quarta to the face

Plate 27

Feint Above the Dagger, Cavazione in Quarta Under the Opponent's Dagger as He Attempts an Upward Parry, and Strike to the Chest

Start in an extended terza with the dagger close to your right wrist, while the opponent is in a low quarta, his sword withdrawn and his dagger high and extended.

Begin the action with a feint in terza above his dagger, without moving your dagger from its current location. As the opponent attempts an upward parry with his dagger and a simultaneous strike in seconda or quarta, perform a cavazione under his dagger and strike him in the chest in quarta. In the same tempo, parry his attack.

Practical Synopsis of Plate 27

- Starting position: agent in extended terza with his dagger near his right wrist, patient in low quarta with his sword withdrawn and his dagger high and extended

1. Agent: in terza and without moving his dagger, performs a feint above the patient's dagger
2. Patient: parries upward with his dagger while in the same tempo attempting to strike the agent in the chest with a quarta or seconda
3. Agent: while parrying patient's attack with his dagger, performs a cavazione below the patient's sword and strikes him in the chest in quarta

Plate 28

Dagger-Parry Under Your Right Arm, and Strike in Seconda to the Opponent's Face or Riverso Stramazzone to His Sword-Arm

Start in a low or high terza, with your dagger near your right wrist. The opponent is in any guard suitable for gaining your sword to the outside.

Start gaining his sword to the outside, in a high or low terza and lifting your dagger according to the situation. If he attempts a cavazione and a strike in quarta or seconda to the inside, do the following. Perform a downward parry with your dagger, under your sword-arm, and deliver a stramazzone to his arm or a thrust in seconda to his face.

Practical Synopsis of Plate 28

- Starting position: to the outside—agent in high or low terza with the dagger near his wrist, patient in any guard suitable for gaining to the outside

1. Agent: starts to gain opponent's sword to the outside in terza (high or low, as needed) and raises his dagger (also as needed)
2. Patient: performs a cavazione to the inside to attack with a quarta or seconda

3a. Agent: parries downward with his dagger below his sword-arm and ripostes with a stramazzone to the patient's sword-arm

3b. Agent: parries downward with his dagger below his sword-arm and delivers a counterthrust to the face in seconda

Plate 29

Strike to the Left Shoulder in Seconda Above the Opponent's Dagger, while He Attempts to Gain Your Sword to the Outside

Start in an extended terza, with your dagger crossed over the near end of your sword's forte. The opponent is in the same position.

If he attempts to gain your sword in terza to the outside, do the following. Perform a cavazione and, in one tempo, beat his blade in quarta, use the dagger to parry his blade (which you have just beaten) and strike him in the same tempo to the left shoulder above his dagger.

Practical Synopsis of Plate 29

- Starting position: to the outside—agent in extended terza with the dagger crossed over the forte, patient in same guard

1. Agent: comes to gain opponent's sword to the outside in terza
2. Patient: performs a cavazione and beats the agent's sword in quarta (beat: right to left); then, uses his dagger to cover the line to his high left, while delivering a thrust to the opponent's left shoulder, above the dagger (hand in seconda)

Plate 30

Feint and Strike in Seconda to the Opponent's Left Shoulder Above His Dagger, Against a Descending Dagger-Parry Under His Right Arm[55]

Start in terza or quarta with your arm withdrawn and your dagger close to your right wrist. The opponent is in quarta with his sword withdrawn and his dagger high and extended.

Perform a feint under his dagger while lifting yours. As he attempts a downward dagger-parry (towards his left), perform a cavazione in the same tempo above his dagger, parry inside with your dagger under your right arm, and strike him in seconda above his dagger.

PRACTICAL SYNOPSIS OF PLATE 30

- Starting position: agent in terza or quarta with the sword-arm withdrawn and the dagger near his wrist, patient in quarta with the sword withdrawn and the dagger high and extended

1. Agent: feints below opponent's dagger and lifts his dagger
2. Patient: attempts a downward dagger-parry to his left side, while thrusting [in terza] to the agent's mid-torso
3. Agent: parries the attack with his dagger (left to right, under his own right arm), while performing a cavazione above the patient's dagger and striking him in seconda to the chest

55 This is an instance where Capoferro's wording is vague and potentially misleading. The opponent's initial guard makes it far more likely that your feint would be under his *left* arm, and that, consequently, it would be under the said left arm that the opponent would perform his downward, right-to-left parry. Also, the patient is illustrated not as he executes the parry described in the text, but likely as he lifts his dagger again, in the attempt to thwart the final thrust.

Plate 31

Left-Foot Pass and Ascending *Punta In Falso*[56] to the Chest Between the Weapons, with an Over-Arm Dagger-Parry, Your Weapons Well-Closed Together

The opponent starts in terza with both weapons extended in an oblique line, so that his sword points to your right shoulder and his dagger to your left shoulder. Face him in terza, with your sword-point low, your dagger high, and your body bent to your left as much as possible.

If he approaches you to gain your sword or to perform another action, do the following. In that tempo, pass with your left foot towards his right, parry with your dagger to the inside over your right arm and deliver an ascending *punta in falso* between his weapons.

Or, you could perform a cavazione with both your weapons and your sword on top, press down on his sword and, in the same tempo, strike him in terza.

Practical Synopsis of Plate 31

- Starting position: agent in terza with weapons extended, blades slightly converging; patient in terza, sword-point low, dagger high and body bent to the left;

1. Agent: approaches to gain the patient's sword [to the inside]

2a. Patient: passes with left foot towards his left, performs a dagger opposition-parry (left to right) above his right arm and strikes the opponent between weapons with an upward *punta in falso*

2b. Patient: passes with his left foot towards his left, performs a cavazione to the outside with both weapons, parries with both weapons (sword on top), and in the same tempo strikes his adversary with an ascending terza while pressing down on his sword-blade

---

56 See paragraph 17 (The Thrust) from The Practice, "Explanation of Some Practical Fencing Terms."

Plate 32

Strike in Quarta to the Throat with a Cavazione and a Low Dagger-Parry as the Opponent Attempts an Attack by Cavazione and a Dagger-Parry

The opponent starts in a high terza, with his dagger crossed over the near end of his sword's forte, and his sword held somewhat at an angle. Gain his sword in terza to the outside, with your dagger high.

When he attempts a cavazione under your sword and a strike in quarta together with a dagger-parry, do this in a single tempo: perform a descending dagger-parry towards your left side, execute a cavazione under his dagger and strike him in quarta to the face or wherever may be more expedient.

Practical Synopsis of Plate 32

- Starting position: to the outside—agent in terza, patient in high terza with his dagger at an angle and joined to the near section of the forte of his angled sword

1. Agent: gains opponent's sword in terza to the outside
2. Patient: performs a cavazione below the agent's sword
3. Agent: parries downward and to the left with his dagger, performs a cavazione below opponent's dagger and strikes him in quarta to the face (or other more convenient target)

Plate 33

Striking in Quarta to the Chest Under the Opponent's Dagger while Executing a Backward Right-Foot Pass and a High Dagger-Parry Against a Passing Attack in Seconda Above Your Dagger

If the opponent is in a low terza, face him in a high terza with your dagger joined to your sword-blade, above the forte.

If he attacks you with a pass in seconda above your dagger while attempting a wide parry with his, pass back with your right foot and, as he lifts his dagger to parry, perform a cavazione under his dagger and strike him in quarta, ensuring that you extend your body forward as pictured.

Practical Synopsis of Plate 33

- Starting position: agent in low terza, patient in high terza with his dagger joined at an angle over his forte

1. Agent: passes forward to attack in seconda above the opponent's dagger, while using his dagger to parry right-to-left
2. Patient: passes back with his right foot, lifts his dagger to parry while performing a cavazione with his sword below the patient's dagger, carrying his body forward to strike in quarta

Plate 34

Striking in Seconda to the Chest Over the Opponent's Dagger Against an Attack with a Pass of the Left Foot. Defending with a Pass Back of the Right Foot and a Dagger-Parry Under the Right Arm

If the opponent is in quarta with his sword low and withdrawn, and with the dagger extended, high and open, face him in quarta with your sword-arm extended and your dagger high.

If he passes forward to attack you in seconda and to parry your sword with his dagger, pass back with your right foot, parry downwards with your dagger (to your right), perform a cavazione over his dagger and strike him in seconda.

PRACTICAL SYNOPSIS OF PLATE 34

- Starting position: agent in quarta with sword low and withdrawn and dagger extended high and open; patient in quarta with the arm extended and dagger high

1. Agent: attacks with a left-foot pass in seconda while executing a downward dagger-parry
2. Patient: passes back with his right foot and executes a left-to-lower-right dagger parry; at the same time, performs a cavazione above opponent's dagger and strikes in seconda

Plate 35

Cavazione Over the Opponent's Dagger and Strike to the Chest, Between the Weapons, while the Opponent is in a *Larga* Guard[57] and Lets You Get in Measure

If the opponent is in quarta with his sword-arm withdrawn, his dagger-arm extended and the dagger high, open and with the blade vertical, face him in an extended terza. Keep your dagger at an angle in front of your chest, and approach him to the outside of his dagger, when he is motionless in his guard.

Once you arrive with your sword-point level with his dagger, perform a cavazione in quarta over his dagger and strike his chest with a lunging thrust.

Practical Synopsis of Plate 35

- Starting position: agent in extended terza with dagger at an angle in front of his chest, patient in quarta with his arm withdrawn and his dagger high and open, blade vertical

1. Agent: approaches opponent to the outside of dagger
2. Patient: does not move
3. Agent: when the point of this sword arrives at the opponent's dagger, performs a cavazione above it and delivers a thrust in quarta to his adversary's chest

[57] A *larga* guard (*guardia larga*) is a guard in which the sword's point is off-line and leaves the body open. It is often used as an invitation.

Plate 36

Fencing with Sword and Cape

To make the subject of sword and cape clearer, it may not be out of context to explain some principles that must be observed with this weapon combination. If you are wearing a cape, let it fall off your right shoulder and down to the middle of your left arm. Then, turn your left hand toward the outside, wrapping the cape around your arm, and set yourself in terza or in any other guard you prefer.

As far as footwork, use the same as you do with the sword and dagger. The steps are the same, save for those associated with the parry, since the cape can be slashed or perforated, which is not the case with the dagger.

So, if you face the opponent in terza (as I said above), and he attacks you with a mandritto to the head, you must pass forward in the same tempo and parry with the cape against his forte while pushing a thrust to his chest.

You can also parry this attack with your sword in prima, in guardia di testa,[58] accompanied by the cape, while pulling your left foot near the right. Then immediately pass forward with your right foot and turn a mandritto to his head or leg.

If he attacks you with a mandritto or riverso to your leg, somewhat withdraw your right foot; if his attack is a mandritto, give him a riverso to the sword-arm, and if it is a riverso, strike him there with a mandritto.

But the best way to parry is with the sword, and to riposte with the sword accompanied by the cape, pressing against his blade, which allows you to operate with confidence.

The illustration shows you how to gain the opponent's sword to the inside with this weapon combination.[59]

---

58 A guard in which the sword is high and angled to the left (point higher or lower than the hilt, depending on source). This guard is often encountered in 16th-century Italian fencing literature as being ideal for parrying cuts to the head.

59 This also shows you the guard of sword and cape. Although a quarta is illustrated, a terza would have roughly the same position of the weapons.

Practical Synopsis of Plate 36

- Starting position: [agent in terza], patient in terza

Sequence A

1. Agent: cuts a mandritto to opponent's head
2. Patient: in the tempo of the cut, passes forward with his left foot, parries with the cape to the opponent's forte while delivering a thrust to the opponent's chest

Sequence B

1. Agent: cuts a mandritto to opponent's head

2a. Patient: while gathering forward with his left foot, parries with his sword in guardia di testa accompanied with his cape; ripostes by stepping forward with his right foot and cutting a mandritto to the opponent's head

2b. Patient: while gathering forward with his left foot, parries with his sword in guardia di testa accompanied with his cape; ripostes by stepping forward with his right foot and cutting a mandritto to the opponent's leg

Sequence C

1. Agent: cuts a mandritto to opponent's leg
2. Patient: pulls his right foot back and counters with a riverso to the patient's sword-arm

Sequence D

1. Agent: cuts a riverso to opponent's leg
2. Patient: pulls his right foot back and counters with a mandritto to the patient's sword-arm

Sequence E (basic)

1. Agent: cuts a mandritto to the opponent's head
2. Patient: executes an inside parry with the sword, and ripostes by thrust or cut wherever open, while maintaining right-to-left opposition with the cape against the opponent's sword

Plate 37

Striking with a Controcavazione in Quarta to the Face, Parrying with the Cape-Arm to the Outside, while the Opponent Performs a Cavazione to Attack You with a Thrust

Your opponent starts in quarta with his sword high and extended. You gain his blade in quarta to the inside, with your cape-arm under your forte.

As he performs a cavazione to launch any sort of thrusting attack, execute an ascending parry with your cape (to the outside of the cape, i.e., to your left), perform a controcavazione in quarta and strike him in the face, or wherever it is more suitable.

Practical synopsis of plate 37

- Starting position: to the inside—agent in quarta with cape-arm below his forte, patient in quarta with sword high and extended

1. Agent: gains the opponent's sword to the inside
2. Patient: performs a cavazione to attack with a thrust to the outside
3. Agent: parries with the cape high and to the left, executes a controcavazione to the inside in quarta and strikes the opponent in face or wherever is most suitable

Plate 38

Striking a Left-Handed Opponent in the Face with a Riverso Stramazzone, or in the Chest with a Seconda or a Quarta to the Outside, as He Performs a Cavazione with the Point of His Sword to Attack

Your left-handed opponent starts in quarta with his sword-arm extended. Begin by gaining his sword in terza to the inside, your dagger high.[60] As he performs a cavazione to attack your face with a seconda, you can strike him in three ways.

You can merely lower your dagger to parry his thrust, and strike his face with a riverso stramazzone. You can alternatively strike him in seconda to the chest. Or, best yet, you can use just your sword and strike his chest in quarta to the outside in the tempo of his cavazione.

[60] Your dagger high: *il pugnale alto la sua spada*. This is a typographical error, making the sentence ambiguous. It could mean "as high as the [yours? his?] sword" or "high."

Practical Synopsis of Plate 38

- Starting position: to the agent's inside —agent in terza with dagger as high as patient's sword,[61] patient in quarta with arm extended

Sequence A

1. Agent: gains the opponent's sword to his inside
2. Patient: performs a cavazione to attack the agent to the face in seconda

3a. Agent: lowers his dagger and parries the opponent's sword, riposting with a riverso stramazzone to the face

3b. Agent: lowers the dagger and parries the opponent's sword, counterthrusting with a seconda to the chest

Sequence B

1. Agent: gains the opponent's sword to his inside
2. Patient: performs a cavazione to attack the agent to the face in seconda
3. Agent: as the opponent performs the cavazione, strikes him to his outside in the chest with a quarta

61 See previous note.

Plate 39

Parrying an Attack to the Head with the Sword-Point High and the Dagger Crossed Under the Forte of the Sword, so that You Can Riposte in Two Ways: with a Thrust to the Face or a Riverso to the Leg

I would do myself an injustice if I omitted this noble parry or defense, which protects an equally noble part of your body.

So, let me offer this illustration, in which the opponent starts in prima, and you in quinta. From the quinta, you only lift your arm and turn your hand in quarta, step forth with your right foot and gain the opponent's sword to the inside. The opponent performs a cavazione under your blade and attacks your head with a mandritto fendente. You merely turn your hand in seconda, keeping your sword-point high, and cross your dagger behind the forte of your sword.

This enables you to riposte confidently in two ways: either with a thrust to the face or with a cut to his leg. These ripostes are represented by the two lines in the illustration coming down from the point of the sword—one to the opponent's head, the other to his thigh.

Practical Synopsis of Plate 39

- Starting position: to the inside—agent in quinta, patient in prima

1. Agent: gains the opponent's sword to the inside by raising his arm and turning his hand in quarta, while widening his stance by stepping forward with the right foot
2. Patient: performs a cavazione below the agent's sword and turns a mandritto fendente [to the opponent's head]

3a. Agent: turns his hand into seconda, raises his point and places his dagger behind his sword against the opponent's forte; then he strikes the opponent with a thrust to the face

3b. Agent: turns his hand into seconda, raises his point and places his dagger behind his sword against the opponent's forte; then he strikes the opponent with a riverso to the leg

Plate 40

Striking the Opponent with a Terza to the Thigh and with a Dagger-Thrust to the Body, Against a Riverso by Cavazione to the Leg

Some may think that the action depicted here, a simultaneous sword- and dagger-strike, is difficult to perform. But if you try it after my explanation, you will find it easy.

Start both with the swords in quarta, with the true edges touching and the points aimed at each other's face. Press against the opponent's blade so that, upon feeling the pressure, he turns a riverso to your leg.[62] Immediately lower your sword, turn your hand in terza, pass forward with your left foot and strike him with your sword and your dagger (while parrying) as shown.

PRACTICAL SYNOPSIS OF PLATE 40

- Starting position: to the inside—both in quarta with true edges touching and the points directed at each others' faces

1. Agent: presses his blade against that of the opponent
2. Patient: feeling the pressure, immediately turns a riverso to the agent's leg
3. Agent: parries by lowering his sword with his hand in terza, passes forward with his left foot and strikes the patient in the flank with his dagger and in the leg with his sword

---

[62] This is a good explanation of a true-edge on true-edge crossing, with pressure coming into play. This is a pivotal concept to understand the narrow play (*gioco stretto*) in 16th-century Italian swordsmanship.

Plate 41

Parrying a Riverso Stramazzone with the Sword, then Passing Forward with the Left Foot and Striking the Opponent Under His Arm with the Dagger

Parrying a thrust with the dagger (to either side) and riposting with a stramazzone riverso to the sword-arm is a widely established technique. So, if he parries your thrust to the inside—i.e., towards your left—and turns the stramazzone, parry with your sword in terza to your outside, pass forward with your left foot, place your dagger above his sword and strike him with a seconda to the chest.

Here is the explanation of this illustration. The opponent is in terza with the dagger over the forte of his sword, while you are in settima[63] with the dagger-arm extended and the sword somewhat low and withdrawn. Once you are in measure, thrust above his dagger. He parries to the outside—i.e., to his left—and ripostes with a riverso stramazzone. Parry this in quarta, pass forward with your left foot and strike him with your dagger as shown. To recover safely, pass back with your left foot and, in the same tempo, deliver a riverso to his sword-arm; then, recover in your initial guard.

[63] Capoferro never illustrates this guard, nor explains its properties; for instance, we are left with no good indication of how this guard is different from the sesta illustrated and designated by the letter F in plate 3.

Practical Synopsis of Plate 41

- Starting position: to the inside—agent in settima with his dagger-arm extended and his sword low and withdrawn, patient in terza with his dagger joined to the forte of his sword

Sequence A

1. Agent: attacks the opponent with a thrust
2. Patient: parries left-to-right with the dagger and ripostes with a riverso stramazzone
3. Agent: parries the attack with his sword in terza; immediately, while placing his dagger above the agent's sword, strikes him in the chest with a thrust in seconda

Sequence B

1. Agent: thrusts over the opponent's dagger
2. Patient: parries right-to-left with his dagger and cuts a riverso stramazzone
3. Agent: parries with the sword in quarta, passes forward with his left foot and strikes the opponent with a dagger-thrust; then, he withdraws his left foot and cuts a riverso to the patient's sword arm, finally recovering into his initial guard

Plate 42

How Best to Use the Rotella Against Another Rotella

When you do not know how to operate it properly, the very weapon you hold can often turn into a warring opponent. This is why I have decided to include a few details on the rotella, a weapon most dangerous to those who do not possess its fundamentals.

Hold the rotella strapped to your left arm, with the arm a little bent, so that the shield faces somewhat to the left. Do not bend your arm so much that the rotella blocks your view and prevents you from seeing any part of the opponent.

Once you are in this position, and you are ready to attack an opponent who is in a *stretta* guard[64] with the sword extended forward, you must first gain his sword to either side, depending on the situation. Then, pass forward with your left foot, press your rotella against the opponent's sword (which you had previously gained with your blade), and strike him with an ascending terza from the wrist.

If the opponent is in a *larga* guard[65] and attacks you with a mandritto or riverso to your leg, parry either blow with a falso and riposte with a cut to his leg.

If he attacks your head or face with a thrust or cut, you can parry with the rotella, as long as the attack is not a feint.

Against a feint, do not parry with the rotella because its weight prevents you from moving as quickly as you could with a targa or buckler. This is what happens to the fencer in the illustration: he tries to parry a thrust to the outside of his rotella, which causes his view to be blocked. This gives his adversary a sufficient opportunity to pass forward with the left foot and strike him in the chest or in his lower torso (pictured), the motion of his sword unseen.

---

64 *Stretta* guard (*guardia stretta*): a guard, typically with the hand in terza or quarta, in which the sword point is in line, as opposed to a *larga* guard, which features the point off-line (as said in the footnote accompanying plate 35).

65 See previous note.

Instead, parry a similar strike with the sword in seconda or quarta (depending on the situation). Then, pass forward with your left foot, hit the opponent's blade with your rotella and strike him with an ascending terza. Doing this will keep you safe.

Practical Synopsis of Plate 42

Sequence A

- Starting position: agent in terza, patient in terza with his sword extended

1. Agent: gains the patient's sword to the inside
2. Patient: does not react
3. Agent: passing forward with the left foot, uses the rotella for opposition against the opponent's sword and delivers an ascending thrust in terza to the opponent's chest

Sequence B

- Starting position: agent in terza, patient in terza

1. Agent: delivers a mandritto to the patient's front leg
2. Patient: parries the cut with the false edge of the sword, and ripostes with a riverso to the agent's leg (with or without an accrescimento of the right foot, as needed)

Sequence C

- Starting position: agent in terza, patient in terza

1. Agent: delivers a riverso to the patient's front leg
2. Patient: parries the cut with the false edge of the sword, and ripostes with a mandritto to the agent's leg (with or without an accrescimento of the right foot, as needed)

Sequence D

- Starting position: agent in terza, patient in terza

1. Agent: attacks the patient with a thrust to the face or mandritto to the head
2. Parries with the rotella (right-to-left opposition) and simultaneously delivers a thrust in terza between the opponent's weapons

Sequence E (the illustrated plate)

- Starting position: agent in terza, patient in terza

1. Agent: feints a thrust (or a mandritto) to the opponent's face, to the outside of the opponent's rotella
2. Patient: lifts his rotella to parry, and counters with a thrust to the opponent's chest (see previous sequence)
3. Agent: eludes the patient's attempted shield-parry with a cavazione to the low line, while parrying the opponent's thrust with his rotella

Sequence F

- Starting position: agent in terza, patient in terza

1. Agent: feints a thrust or mandritto to the opponent's face
2. Patient: parries the thrust with the sword, hand in quarta, and ripostes with a thrust to the opponent's chest while performing right-to-left opposition with the rotella

Sequence G

- Starting position: agent in terza, patient in terza

1. Agent: feints a riverso to the opponent's face
2. Patient: parries the feint with the sword, hand in seconda, and ripostes with an overhand thrust to the opponent's chest while performing left-to-right opposition with the rotella

Plate 43[66]

Strike Under the Rotella while the Opponent Attempts to Parry with It and Strike You with a Thrust

Always exercise caution when fighting your opponent, by virtue of the feints and deceptions that abound in the art of arms. This illustration shows how, most of the time, a parry is harmful to the fencer who attempts it—that is, when the parry is not accompanied by a riposte in the same tempo. Such is the instance in this situation of sword and rotella.

The opponent is in quinta, with the arm sloping downward, the point of the sword low and the rotella in front of his chest. You are in sesta, with your shield-arm extended forward and your sword somewhat withdrawn. Once in measure, thrust at his face to the outside of his rotella; he will lift his shield to parry, thus obstructing his view, at which you will perform a cavazione under his rotella and strike him in the face with a thrust in quarta.

---

66 Note that E and F are reversed in the illustration.

A more sensible opponent would parry the first thrust by extending his shield-arm; he would pass forward with his left foot, bend his body and head to his right and deliver a thrust to your chest. He could also parry the first thrust with his sword (in quarta), then immediately pass forward with his left foot, hit your blade with his shield and deliver an ascending thrust to your chest. This would keep him safe.

Practical Synopsis of Plate 43

- Starting position: agent in quinta with the forearm at a downward angle and the rotella in front of his chest, patient in sesta with his rotella extended forward and the sword somewhat withdrawn

Sequence A

1. Agent: thrusts to the opponent's face on the outside of his rotella
2. Patient: raises his rotella to parry, somewhat obscuring his view
3. Agent: performs a cavazione under the patient's rotella, striking him in the chest with a quarta

Sequence B

1. Agent: thrusts to the opponent's face on the outside of his rotella

2a. Patient: parries the thrust by extending his rotella-arm, passing forward with his left foot and bending his body and head to his right; delivers a thrust to the agent's chest

2b. Patient: parries the thrust with his sword in quarta, then passes forward with his left foot and hits into the agent's sword with his rotella while striking with an ascending thrust in terza

Some Principles Regarding the Cut

I had thought of adding some illustrations on how to deliver and parry cuts (plus a good number of actions on this topic), but I realized I can accomplish the same with a brief discussion of the following principles.

If the opponent is in terza or quarta with the point aimed at the center of your body, face him in quarta, with the point of your sword rather high and angled to your right. As you approach the opponent's sword, cut a mandritto to his blade accompanied by a riverso fendente to the face.

When it is the opponent who turns a riverso to your face, pass and parry with your dagger in guardia di faccia (over your right arm), delivering a thrust in terza to his chest. After parrying, you could also pass and deliver a mandritto to his leg. Alternatively, you can parry with your sword in quarta, as you see in the illustration where you are directed to strike the opponent with the dagger under his arm.[67] By passing and parrying with the dagger, you can strike the opponent with a riverso to the leg, or even with the dagger (as we have seen) under his arm.

You could also face him in quarta with the point of your sword low, offering an opening with your body; as he comes to the outside to attack you with a thrust, parry upwards with your false edge and strike him with a mandritto to the face or with a thrust to the chest.

If the opponent attempts to beat your sword to the inside or outside, this is how you must proceed. If he delivers a mandritto to your sword, in the same tempo turn a riverso to his face. If he delivers a riverso to the outside to beat your sword, in the same tempo, turn a mandritto to his face.

Parry a mandritto or riverso to the head as you have been taught by the illustration showing the defense with the sword and dagger crossed—the dagger crossed behind the sword's forte. That illustration has two lines, one descending to the face, the other to the thigh.[68]

If the opponent attacks your lower parts with a mandritto or riverso, parry in seconda with your point low. After parrying a mandritto, perform a tight cavazione[69] above his sword, place your dagger over his blade and deliver a riverso to his arm. Against a low-line riverso, parry in the same manner (but to the outside) and strike him in the chest with a thrust, making sure that you place your dagger over his sword in the same tempo.

This is all I needed to say concerning this topic.

67 Plate 41.

68 Plate 39.

69 *Cavazione di filo*. See footnote accompanying plate 12.

A Failsafe Way to Defend Against Any Attack by Parrying with a Riverso and Always Striking with an Imbroccata

As I get ready to finish this work, I think it may be useful to end it with a brief dissertation that illustrates the virtues of the prima and quarta guards. The prima strikes the opponent while the quarta defends against him—the beginning and the end of any honorable quarrel. The quarta defends against any attack (feint or earnest), while the prima strikes the opponent.

It is, however, important to remark that these two guards are inseparable companions, and that one ends where the other begins; in other words, they begin and end without an actual beginning or end.

The prima starts high and ends in quarta rather low, and this for two reasons. Firstly, if the opponent attacks you with a thrust or a cut, you can parry with a riverso while passing with your left foot somewhat towards the opponent's right side; you can then push your right foot forward and strike him with an imbroccata to the chest, at the end of which you would again be in quarta. Secondly, the opponent would only be able to attack your right side, which makes it easy to defend with an ascending cut from the quarta.

Make sure you perform these actions with a brave countenance and an eye quick to spot where the opponent is open and where he is well defended. Also, make sure you have strength and readiness in your legs, arms and hands, swiftness to parry and strike, and agility in your body.[70]

This is the nature of the prima and quarta guards.[71]

70 Brave[ry], strength, readiness, swiftness, agility. *Ardimento, fortezza, prontezza, prestezza, agilita'.* This is a variation on the theme of the virtues required of a swordsman as far back as Italy's earliest-extant fencing treatise, that of Fiore de' Liberi (circa 1410).

71 The action described here is a well-known "universal parry and riposte" often advocated in the 16th century, by authors such as Angelo Viggiani (1575).

Glossary of Common and Useful Italian Rapier Fencing Terms

Please note that the following explanations assume right-handed fencers. Also, the list of examples referencing Capoferro's text is not meant to be exhaustive, as too many of these principles occur a high number of times throughout the *Gran Simulacro.*

Accrescimento – A forward motion of the front foot. If this is performed from the ordinary stance, it puts you in the extraordinary stance, which, in the course of an attack, is the equivalent position to that of a fencing lunge (see plate 5).

Arms of the hilt – The semi-circular elements of the hilt that extend on either side of the blade from just under the hilt's quillons and along the plane of the blade.

Beat – 1) A percussive cut executed against the opponent's blade (e.g., plate 16, sequence B, or plate 19, sequence C). 2) A smart tap on the ground executed with the front foot (in Classical fencing, an *appel*), as Capoferro mentions in plate 20.

Brutish man (*uomo bestiale*) – This is one of the many designations of an instinctive brawler, as opposed to a fencer who knows and fences by the rules of the art. From the *Büffel* (buffalo) of the German Liechtenauer tradition, through the *uomo bestiale* of Capoferro's day, to Classical fencing's *tiratore* (instinctive player), the brutish man has permeated fencing history as an unpredictable opponent against whom, at times, special tactics must be used. Not to be confused with the choleric man (one of four temperaments sometimes discussed in fencing treatises), since perfect knowledge of fencing can coexist in the latter alongside aggressiveness.

Cavazione – 1) A thrusting attack incorporating a spiral motion of your blade from one side of the opponent's weapon to the other, done predominantly after the opponent gains your blade or while he is in the process of doing so. 2) A semi-circular motion of your blade from one side of the opponent's weapon to the other, done to free your sword from his and to gain his blade. Plate 7 is the first of countless examples of this action used offensively.

Circular parry (*affrontare la spada*) – A simple parry preceded by a tight cavazione around the opponent's blade. In Capoferro, this happens predominantly from the inside to the outside, and is followed by a riposte to the flank under the opponent's blade. Examples of this action in Capoferro may be found in plates 13, 15 and 17.

Contratempo – In Capoferro, an attack that takes the tempo from the opponent's taking a step to gain your blade (described in The Practice, paragraph 10; example: plate 29). Also in Capoferro, as well as in general 17th-century fencing theory, the deliberate creation of a tempo to lure the opponent to attack, so that his action may be defeated by a defense and counterthrust in single tempo (described in Explanation of Some Practical Fencing Terms, paragraph 3; example: plate 14).

Controcavazione – The act of nullifying the opponent's cavazione by performing one of your own. Capoferro describes its use in plate 15, while plate 37 has an example of this technique in action.

Counterthrust – A thrust executed in the same tempo as the opponent's attack. The vast majority of the actions in Capoferro and contemporaries feature counterthrusts.

Cut – An offensive action using the percussive and shearing abilities of the blade to inflict injury on the opponent.

Dagger and cape parries – The canonic dagger parries (with simultaneous counterthrust) in Italian rapier are four: 1) high, right-to left, with counterthrust in quarta; 2) low, right-to-left, with counterthrust in quarta; 3) left-to-right over the right arm, with counterthrust in terza; 4) left-to-right under the right arm, with counterthrust in seconda or prima. The first, third, and fourth are the most used, and are also often employed as cape parries.

Debole – The half of the blade containing the point, and ideal for the offense.

Dominating the sword – Controlling the opponent's blade. Capoferro states that it can be done either by gaining the opponent's sword and not relinquishing the advantage until you attack, or by executing a beat. Capoferro devotes a paragraph to this technique in The Practice.

Extraordinary stance – The distance between your feet when it is wider than the ordinary stance. This is also the stance your feet assume at the maximum extension of a fencing lunge (see plate 5 for an illustration of this stance).

False edge – The edge of the sword that faces up when the weapon is sheathed at your side.

Falso – A cut executed with the false edge. This is generally done almost vertically; when left-to-right, it is called *falso manco*, when right-to-left, *falso dritto*.

Feint – A simulated attack designed to draw a parry from your opponent, which you then elude by means of a cavazione. Although stating a dislike for this principle in the first part of The Practice, Capoferro makes ample use of it throughout the action plates, starting with plate 7, sequence B.

Forte – The half of the blade adjacent the hilt, and ideal for the defense.

Gaining the sword (finding the sword, *stringere*) – Placing your blade against the opponent's so that a) the two weapons meet at a point closer to your forte than to his and b) he cannot attack you without first performing a cavazione. An excellent illustration of this example in single sword may be seen in plate 15 (figure C gaining figure D's blade).

Guard – 1) A posture of your weapon, body, and feet that maximizes your defensive and offensive capabilities. 2) A position of the sword-hand (see prima, seconda, terza, or quarta).

Guardia di faccia – A guard commonly described in 16th-century Italian swordsmanship treatises, consisting of the parrying weapon being extended at face-level towards the opponent. This was considered ideal for parrying cuts to the face, while also creating a threat. Capoferro mentions this guard in the chapter "Some Principles Regarding the Cut."

Guardia di testa – A guard commonly described in 16th-century Italian swordsmanship treatises, consisting of the sword being held with the hilt at shoulder-level, arm extended, and the blade at a rightward lateral angle in protection of the head. This was considered ideal for parrying cuts to the head. Capoferro uses this guard in plate 36.

High line – One of the four main lines in Italian rapier. When the opponent's blade is below yours, you are on the high line.

Imbroccata – An overhand thrust executed with the hand in prima. Capoferro describes its use as an universal riposte in his last chapter.

Incascio – The semicircular space between the inside arm of the hilt and the ricasso of the blade. This is the space through which the index finger of the sword-hand is inserted to properly grip the weapon in the Italian style.

Inquartata – A void and counterthrust generally consisting of crossing your left foot behind your right, while forming strong opposition in quarta to the inside line. Plate 19 (figure C) is a good example of this technique.

Inside – One of the four main lines in Italian rapier. When the opponent's blade is to the left of yours, you are on the inside.

Low line – One of the four main lines in Italian rapier. When the opponent's blade is above yours, you are on the low line. Also, the low line is assumed for all attacks to the flank or cuts to the legs.

Larga (wide) Guard – A guard in which the point of your sword is directed low or away from the opponent.

Lunge – A thrusting attack that incorporates an accrescimento of the right foot, and in which the limbs and body act in concert to produce the longest possible reach and a strong forward momentum, while offering as little target as possible to the opponent. The illustration in Capoferro's plate 5 is one of fencing history's most celebrated examples of this technique. Note: in Capoferro's time, the general Italian term for this was *distesa* or *botta lunga* (the latter giving the modern term its etymology).

Mandritto – A cut proceeding right-to-left, literally "forehand."

Mandritto fendente – A mandritto proceeding downwards almost vertically.

Mandritto tondo – A mandritto proceeding horizontally.

Measure – The distance between two opposing fencers. Capoferro classifies measures in slightly confusing ways. In general, though, measure can be wide (needing a lunge to reach the opponent), narrow (needing only a forward extension of the body to reach the opponent) or narrowest (closer than narrow).

Narrow stance – A stance in which your feet are closer together than in the ordinary stance.

Opposition – 1) An obtuse angle between the sword-arm and the sword designed to keep the opponent's weapon to the side or otherwise incapable of threatening you with its point. 2) In less strict terms, a small pressure exerted against the opponent's weapon in the course of your attack, riposte, or counterthrust. Note: as a term, "opposition" did not appear until the Classical era (late 18th century), although other words such as "parry" were used in Capoferro's day. You can see a rather extreme example of high-line opposition in plate 10, by figure D, or a regular example of opposition in quarta to the inside in plate 19 (figure C).

Ordinary stance – A stance in which your feet are approximately one-and-a-half shoe-lengths apart. You can see that in plate 5 as the line designated D.

Outside – One of the four main lines in Italian rapier. When the opponent's blade is to the right of yours, you are on the outside.

Palmo – A unit of measure often used in fencing: the distance between the tip of the thumb and little fingers of the hand when comfortably stretched near maximum reach. Capoferro uses it often in conjunction with his description of gaining the opponent's blade.

Parry – Generally, a defense against an attack from the opponent, using the sword, a companion weapon or even the left hand. Also, the word used in period fencing literature to describe opposition, before the term was introduced.

Pass – A piece of footwork in which the rear foot goes in front of the front foot (as in natural walking) or vice-versa. It can also be used in the course of an attack, in lieu of an accrescimento of the front foot (or lunge). Examples of this type of offensive footwork may be found in plates 9 (figure D), 11 (figure C), 12 (figure D), and many others. Lastly a backward pass may also be used offensively to thwart an attack while giving yourself more room and time to react, as you can see in plate 33 (figure C), or to void an attack against the front leg (plate 8, figure D).

Pressing the blade – Applying pressure to the opponent's blade, generally to provoke a cavazione. An example of the use of this technique in Capoferro may be found in plate 40.

Pressing the opponent – Advancing on the opponent to keep him on the defensive (Italian *stringere la vita*).

Prima – A guard or hand-position in which the sword-hand is higher than the shoulder, the true edge facing up, natural opposition to the high line. Capoferro designates it with the letter A.

Punta in falso – An ascending thrust with the hand in terza. Plate 31 (figure F) shows an example of this attack.

Punta riversa – A thrust executed with the hand in quarta, with opposition markedly to the inside line. Capoferro describes it in paragraph 17 of Explanation of Some Practical Fencing Terms, and mentions it again in plate 24.

Quarta – A guard or hand-position in which the sword-hand is usually at chest-level or lower, the true edge facing left, natural opposition to the inside line. Capoferro designates it with the letter D.

Quillons – The crossguard of the hilt.

Quinta – The fifth guard illustrated by Capoferro and designated with the letter E. It features the forearm sloping down with the blade, and the dagger joined to the forte of the sword, which is held rather withdrawn. It is not described in detail, nor does it appear by this name in contemporary fencing literature.

Ricasso – The thickest part of the blade going from the quillons to about a palmo along the blade.

Riposte – An "answer" (literally) to the opponent's attack in the form of an attack of your own, at the same time or immediately following your parry.

Riverso – A cut proceeding left-to-right, literally a "backhand."

Riverso ascendente – A riverso proceeding low-to-high. Capoferro describes its virtues as an universal parry in his last chapter.

Riverso fendente – A riverso proceeding almost vertically high-to-low.

Riverso tondo – A riverso proceeding horizontally.

Scannatura – Most likely, a thrusting action in which the target is gone through lengthwise. An example may be seen in plate 13.

Seconda – A guard or hand-position in which the sword-hand is generally at shoulder-height, true edge facing right, natural opposition to the outside. Capoferro designates it with the letter B.

Seconda-terza – A guard in which the sword-hand is situated half-way between the seconda and the terza. It is the hand-position ideal for gaining the opponent's sword to the outside.

Sesta – The sixth guard illustrated by Capoferro, and designated with the letter F. It features the sword low and withdrawn, and the dagger high and extended. It is not described at length, nor does it appear by the same name in other treatises of the time.

Settima – The seventh guard mentioned, but not illustrated, by Capoferro. It must have looked similar to the sesta, perhaps with the dagger not has high. It is not described at length, nor does it appear by the same name in other treatises of the time. Capoferro mentions it in the text accompanying plate 41.

Simple parry – A parry not incorporating a simultaneous counterthrust, and requiring a riposte in a subsequent (second) tempo. An example of that may be found in plate 39 (figure E).

Stance – The distance between your feet while on guard or performing a fencing action.

Stramazzone – A cut executed with a circular motion of the wrist, which generally falls like a mandritto or riverso fendente. Examples of stramazzoni can be found in plates 8 (figure D), 28 (figure C) or 38 (figure C).

Stretta (narrow) guard – A guard in which the point of the sword is directed straight at the opponent.

Step – A piece of footwork. Note: the Italian for "step" is *passo,* which is also synonymous with "stance."

Tempo – 1) A unit of fencing time, that temporally measures a motion or stillness in the course of an action. 2) A favorable moment to strike the opponent or to gain an advantage over him. Capoferro discusses the theory of tempo in chapter V of The Art, and lists the tempi commonly taught as favorable moments to strike in paragraph 5 of Explanation of Some Practical Fencing Terms.

Terza – A guard or hand-position in which the hand is at chest-level or lower, true edge facing down, natural opposition to the low line. Capoferro designates it with the letter C.

Terza-quarta – A guard in which the hand is situated half-way between the terza and the quarta. This is the ideal guard in which to gain the opponent's sword to the inside.

Thrust – An offensive action in which the penetrative power of the sword-point is used to inflict injury on the opponent.

True edge – The edge of the sword facing down when the weapon is carried sheathed at your side.

Void – An action designed to make the opponent's attack miss its mark, generally by removing the part being attacked from the path of the offending weapon. This is generally accomplished through footwork, through bending the body in various ways, or through pulling away the limb being attacked. Examples of voids are in plates 8 (figure D), 17 (figure C) or 19 (figure C).

9780982591192